W9-BWO-445

HEAVEN

HEAVEN

EMERSON WHITNEY

McSWEENEY'S

SAN FRANCISCO

McSWEENEY'S
SAN FRANCISCO

ISBN: 978-1-944211-76-9

10 9 8 7 6 5 4 3 2 1

www.mcsweeneys.net

Printed in Canada

For my mom

I.

Mom was sweaty and the one lamp at her side lit the sweat. The light was making shadows that looked like children. She pulled the sheets up to her chin, shut her eyes. A ruddy, unshaven Texan skulked around. His belly hung over his pants, he was looking out one of the windows behind her bed, shaking a fist at her in his mind. Mom sunk deeper into the mattress, her arms folded over her chest. The man, pacing by the bed, waved an open bible at her. She didn't take it—she wasn't sure who he was, why she was barely clothed in bed, why there was a brace around her ribcage, a plastic ID band on her wrist, why it was so hot, so cold, why the sun had already set.

She didn't understand this part: he found her with a few broken ribs and a bloodshot eye, her head against a steering wheel, a thin, blonde woman with little wrists and small hoop earrings, vodka bottles clinking in the well beneath the driver's seat. She looked expensive. He carried her like a blanket back to his bed.

His mother, a cherry-faced German-Texan, came over to watch. This was Old Texas like in the movies, the delirium tremens in Texas, where dip tins make circles in everybody's back pocket. The old woman watched over her like she would a snake, a fire. As if she were on a porch or in a breezeway and not in a humid room, watching a rich-looking white woman shake herself almost to death. The cherry-faced woman knitted in a broken chair next to the bed. This went on for almost ten days, cicadas crowing, bluebells popping up. I like this story. The story of these strangers watching my mom, doing my job. I imagined it. I wasn't there. At the time, I didn't know where she was. We hadn't spoken. I'd been everywhere by then. She was still in Dallas—at least, I figured she was. I told myself I couldn't give a shit less. Mom's probably dead or dying, I'd say. And this was true, at least, mostly. She scared me. Loving her scared me. Eventually, I heard pieces of this story and invented the rest: she was in Texas. There was some guy. There were broken ribs. I had cut off all contact, was on my own. I didn't care about her anymore, I'd say. I'd already grieved.

But then I began to get phone calls from relatives saying she was skidding, maybe to a stop. She wasn't well. They had no idea that

I had started falling, sliding somewhere myself. Everything I fear in her lives hot inside of me. Ask me about my mother now, and I'll answer you with a question. Which of these are my words:

I will be at walmart this aft... goin to the tractor supply and mcdonalds 4 my bday haha u gotta luv the simple life we have another noreaster comin. Can we talk 2moro? I have the day off and I'm usin it to train kitty to pee and poop in the toilet.

Sometime after the broken ribs and the guy with the bible, she moved into a camper parked on the periphery of a graveyard. The camper was '70s-style with white plastic paneling and a red racing stripe. It was pulled under a group of poplar trees, which leaned heavy across an ornate wrought-iron fence and scratched the roof. When she'd walk outside on her way anywhere she'd squish across repotted grass, over blown headstones that her boyfriend was supposed to fix.

Every day, she checked her teeth in a tiny mirror over her stove, poured a cup of coffee, and stepped outside. The camper door slapped. She walked into town through the tourists, through the side door to the inn where she worked. She took this walk six days a week with her head down, wiping her hands on her apron. The skin of her palms peeled off, peeling from bleaching bathtubs and sinks.

* * *

My mother looks like a woman from New York City anyway, even with broken skin. She is proud of a gap in her teeth where she didn't pay for a new tooth, where she gums at watery candy now, she says. Her shoulders and hands are torn up, but the fan of her neck is always powdered or moisturized or whatever it is. Her hair is always newly dyed, her face peeks out from the freshness of it, her hands are mostly clasped in her lap, her eyes darting all around.

When I was little, I'd twist her hair around my hand and hold it. She'd put her head into my stomach, knees pressed into the linoleum, wearing jeans and a gray sweatshirt with the elastic worn out. She'd make wet streaks on my shirt, sobbing so her head bounced against my stomach, wild and hard, her nose running down.

I'd put my hands on the back of her head, she'd whimper. I'd hold her hair.

I'd miss her so much even though she was right there. Miss her like a sheath. Her blue eyes would beat into mine. A tear would kick off my face and onto her head. Mom would see it, reach up and touch it.

I am like Mom. Symmetrical and tan. I write about her body because of my own discomfort, the oil drum fire that is myself.

I want you to see this: Mom looks like Grace Kelly, blonde and summery, she looks steep, lithe, a proud woman with missing teeth. The truth is in her mouth. The etymology of woman is wife.

When I was little, I held a responsibility to her and we were meant to be women, her eyes drawing me down. I wanted to cup her to my cheek. Everyone watched her. I felt that attention as heat. I came alive when I realized this responsibility, I was so young that there wasn't really language for it.

I saw this meme the other day that read: "This is such a deep... deep memory... I almost can't tell if it's real," and the photo was of a tub of these little multicolor plastic bears in seated positions, the blue one felt familiar. Seeing it, I had the sensation they were talking about, a sensation of a memory more than anything else. The bears ("Three Bear Family Counters" on Amazon) are suggested for ages three and up, learning "early math fun."

The writer Stephen J. Smith, in "Physically Remembering Childhood," explains that the way we speak about the body disconnects it from the mind. "It is *my body, your body,* and sadly, a *nobody*... our everyday language creates a forgetfulness of what it might mean to be embodied."

Apparently pre-verbal memories get lost in the transition to language. There's a lot of writing about it, that memories unhooked from language show up as this *sense*. Before three years old, it's sort of like this: we're embodying experience without pinning it to anything. The bear meme works because all of us who were given the toy at three, as suggested, were sorting our insides out. The memory shows up as physical—the etymology of -em is "to put into," like poured into a frame.

I felt this: Mom treated me like I was grown and like her body was mine. I can still find this memory. It's thick and drawn out. She belonged to me because she wanted me to know: our nakedness and the stuff of it traps us together, this is permanent, her eyes said.

I used to watch Mom on TV, would pull the videos out of the back of the cupboard while I was home sick as a teenager, they were in green VHS sleeves, in the way back. I don't know where they are now and it doesn't matter because nobody has a VCR. A blonde man and woman sat forward in heavy floral chairs. They chatted, glanced at the camera from the foreground of a pastel painting of Sacramento, the woman's shoulder pads blotting out the American River. The woman turned to face the camera, she said Marie.

A craft-scene backdrop slapped onto the screen. A blue wall. The camera panned to Mom behind a brown table filled with scraps of things, paper. She was perfect and '80s, had giant red glasses. She blinked at the camera, held up a cutout of my image that she'd made into a lampshade. I was adorable as a lampshade, was four or something years old.

In the photo Mom was holding, I wore overalls and a pink baseball cap. My hands were in my pockets. I looked a little pissed.

She was saying something about my dad, said *Dad* flatly, and I was surprised to hear it. She showed the audience how to make a calendar for kids to understand visitation when their parents were divorced, she moved the cut-out of me to Monday, Wednesday. I never saw Dad like she was talking about, we didn't have a schedule and we didn't live close. She talked about me and explained decoupage, her hair was clipped behind her head, glasses leaning off her nose, beautiful. She made perfect sense.

When the show was live, I'd watch it from a car seat in the living room, I was four, the shadow of a palm tree moving across the floor. I rocked in the car seat with my arms crossed. There was nothing in the room, just foam-green carpet and a bucket of paint at the entry to the kitchen, white paint that smelled empty. I don't know why there was only a car seat.

All those times that Mom's face was center on TV, I waited for her wave. I'd watch her voice, her body, projecting, moving onto its toes. She'd hold her elbow up and smile at the studio audience. I'd wave back. Music would come on, synth-y music about

Sacramento, the crush of light in the living room would make the screen too white, her face and her waving would career off into an advertisement, leave the echo of her voice in the room like paint.

I'd push myself out of the car seat, pad into the kitchen, tip a chair on its back two legs and drag it toward the refrigerator. I always used the same chair, the one with the loose cushion, tan and wrinkled. I'd hoist myself onto the seat, always an inch or two too short to be eye level with the top, would open the fridge and lodge my foot between the interior racks, and use that fulcrum to pull my pacifier off the fridge, the blue one, the one with the elephant on the tip. They stuck it up there so I'd stop sucking on it. I'd stand on the chair totally triumphant, shove it into my mouth with both hands, smile behind it.

When I was an infant, I'd put my mouth around Mom's actual nipple and my face would fill with snot. A red, pimply ring would grow where my mouth was. I gave Mom mastitis, was allergic to her milk. I was allergic to formula, too, to everything, I coughed.

My younger brothers drank her up, when she'd come into the house, they'd feel her breasts arriving. They'd shriek and run toward her legs. I'd hang back. Her smell would rush at me anyway. Light would shift in the house, Mom's voice flickered against the clicking on of lamps. Here's the etymology:

Mammary is a word that's likely derived from a natural sound in baby talk, perhaps imitative of the sound made while sucking—*ma*.

The ache of wanting is enormous. I drank off the plug like a drunk. I'm not ashamed.

Mama is from 1707; *mum* is from 1823; *mummy* in this sense is from 1839; *mommy*, 1844; *momma*, 1852; and *mom*, 1867.

And *mastectomy*, or the surgical removal of a breast, is from 1909, from Greek's *mastos*, like masticate, burn. It's like the "splitting of rocks or gems," from *cleavage*—to cut along a fissure line.

I'm thinking about giving an account of myself.

"The stories do not capture the body to which they refer. Even the history of this body is not fully narratable," Judith Butler writes. "Any effort to 'give an account of oneself' will have to fail in order to approach being true."

Here's a clear failure: there's always an urgency around my portrait.

When I had boobs, the dudes I'd get naked with would say, Wow, so ethnic. I had one guy who'd call them my "Nat Geo boobs." They'd rub their finger across my areola when they said it, big and brown and dripping. It was fucked up and I was proud, too, because everyone told me they came from my grandmother's body. I cut them off years ago now. I don't read the same anymore. In the process, my nipples got spotty, brown and pink, and I shake my shoulders. They're gone into this kind of skin confetti that I don't understand, chewing gum nipples, my friend says, wrinkled and weird. I shut a door.

Now I am not passing. My attempt to write this history falters. Are body parts passed down? Grammy always wants to hand me the negatives of things: she doesn't want me to have kids, she doesn't want me to cook, she tries to toss me a kind of freedom she never had. My maternal line is wives and widows who cleaned banks at night. Grammy wanted to be a cruise ship stewardess and travel, she got married instead. Her inability to retire grates on her—I'm never able to stop cooking lunch for your grandpa, fifty years of lunches and not one day off, she always says and she means every meal every day.

I love this woman for throwing me into deep water. She wants to hoist me up every once in a while and look. My heritage is her hopefulness and the complexity of a body that looks, in parts, like hers.

The last time I visited, Grammy called me to her bedside, she was sitting on the edge of her bed about to take a nap, and she asked me to hand her a plastic CVS bag on the floor—I got you this, she said, rummaging through it. She pulled out a black box with a clear plastic cover, a facial hair remover called Flawless. I don't even know how it does the removing, says it has a built-in LED light: "discreet." There's a full moon on the cover and it boasts an "18-karat gold plated" head. The video on their website says it uses German-engineered technology to fit a hair remover inside a lipstick container. You can use it when "unwanted hairs pop up out of nowhere," the video says. At the end, there's footage of somebody carefully rubbing the lipstick container in circles on a blown-up, peach-colored balloon in a demonstration of gentleness. It honestly looks fun. I didn't want to use it on my face—my toes, maybe, but my chin hairs have been growing forever and I like letting them.

I said, Thanks, but I like to touch my chin hairs when I think and she laughed and was like, Okay, whatever, like, You're so funny. She tugged a second Flawless out of the bag, Got one for myself, too, she said, because she was trying to help.

This is the question of my body and my story about it: is it just mine? I imagine that these hairs or these boobs are exclusively mine somehow, that the scars or the hairs are unique to me, and it's not true. The only thing I'm doing any different from my grandmother is leaving the hairs there, it's the opposite with the boobs. I could just remove the hairs like I did the boobs, or Grammy and I could together.

I notice a crashing in my chest, the slap of belonging, it's a rocking that dislodges all the time—I want to relate to the clicking in my joints and the skipping record of my person. I want to relate to it like sounds of people smoking cigarettes on the corner, a lighter flicking on and off, noise like birds, maybe.

I don't particularly like how I look, but this doesn't constitute any-thing. My thighs meet in a way I find totally objectionable, like a heart with the point as my ankles, though I am satisfied with myself sometimes, and know what beauty feels like when it crosses me, subtle, like folding a quilt.

Really, I can't explain myself without making a mess.

Butler goes on to suggest that we've always already failed at giving this account of ourselves in part because we didn't ask for the language we use (the one or several that we've had to shuffle ourselves into) or the condition of being addressed in that lan-guage, and so we're already lacking control from the start.

Similarly, no one asked for the framework of male and female or the aggregate of gender that we're funneled through. I wonder all the time how much of my identity is influenced by woman-ness or attempts at woman-ness and the way it was passed to me. We're all handed a responsibility. Here's gender: "woman" as a category is fraught, and entire groups have been denied access. "Could we, in fact, release the category of woman from its fixity and white nor-mativity?" writes Saidiya V. Hartman, about "the name 'woman'" and what it "designate[s]," in *Scenes of Subjection.*

I'm interested in what genderqueer Korean American artist and writer Johanna Hedva suggests in their writing on womanhood and disability. Hedva expands the meaning of "woman" to include all oppressed peoples ("the un-cared for, the secondary, the oppressed, the non-, the un-, the less-than") because as it stands, the term doesn't suffice. In their article "Sick Woman Theory," published in *Mask* magazine, Hedva writes that "the identity of 'woman' has erased and excluded many (especially women of color and trans and genderfluid people)."

The photo accompanying the article shows a gathered-up Hedva in a flowing red dress, black lipstick, black beads, pill bottles billowing out from underneath one arm. In Hedva's alternate use of the word, *woman* functions as "a strategic, all-encompassing embrace."

Hedva lets the word, like any word, move around.

Woman doesn't mean a body.

You know, I was going through my things the other day and I found a photo of you that looked just like Ingrid Bergman, my grandma said a few visits ago. She shook her head. I had to look at it twice, you looked just like Ingrid Bergman.

You're biased, I said, I'm just symmetrical.

She laughed, hung her elbows off the end of the bed. She looked down at the carpet, moved it with her toe.

I was staying in this room that is really a closet-sized space attached to hers. Every night before bed, she'd change into a nightgown then come into my room, lean against my bed, hang her arms off the frame. She would chat with me before I went to sleep.

I'm thirty-three. This is still routine. I knotted the covers over the emptiness in my chest and smiled, afraid that she'd try to tuck me in and brush the lack in my clinging sleep T-shirt, wonder where my boobs went. I haven't told her and it's been almost ten years.

As a kid, I'd play with the bigness of her biceps, fascinated by how it swung. I'd hug her and fall into her cleavage, called her Boo-bers. She called me Boobettes as soon as mine grew. This was our bond. No one else in the family had her eyes and no one else had her boobs, I don't know why anyone thought it was appropriate to make this a topic of conversation, but it regularly was. I'd curl my shoulders in to make them less of a thing. I only brought my shoulders back around Grammy, all proud.

At the end of my bed, Grammy looked like everything about me, older. I loved her there, pinching my toes, talking to me like she used to when I lived with her, first as an infant for a few years, and then again for three years starting from the time I was eight. She adjusted my quilt. There were cars braking and moving outside, a line of summer cars headed to hotels. The room smelled like baby powder and warm vacuum, clean carpet. Night was always lit by her snores. I readied for her breath.

I was wondering, Grammy said, looking up at me. Have you ever wondered... I mean, do you think you're like this because your mom likes your brothers more?

My feet tightened. She looked at me with our eyes, a thudding green, everyone else's are brown or blue. In there was so much worry, a wealth of earnest worry as she hung her arms over the end of the bed. She'd been frustrated with me about stereotypical things, she didn't like that I wore baggy clothes or wanted a men's scarf once as a gift. She's not all that femme-presenting herself, so my sense was that whatever she'd been told to do, she was telling me too. We had a tradition of dissecting our family's relationships, she and I spent so much time alone over the years and we'd process. Grammy asking about my brothers was a gesture like checking the engine, she'd stuck the metal rod in the oil and pulled it out, was looking at the level aloud with me. She tightened her mouth when she was done looking and nodded. This is how I took it: your mom fucked up and that fuckup made you you.

I took a breath. She said, I don't know why I asked. Don't worry about it, it's time for bed.

I won't be able to sleep, I figured.

Her arm swished as she pinched my toe. I love you, she said, walking toward the door. She paused with her hand on it, looked back at me.

No one asks about the root causes of heterosexuality or cisgenderism, said Karen Barad, a physicist who was talking to me about Donna Haraway's cyborg theory. (According to Haraway, "cyborg politics is the struggle for language and the struggle against perfect communication, against the one code that translates all meaning perfectly, the central dogma of phallogocentrism.") Yet, it seems like we're forever stuck whirling around the idea that queerness was caused.

There's this graphic illustration of queer theory that I'm teaching right now and in it, there's a fun drawing of bald Michel Foucault in a leather jacket. The illustration has a starry "nature vs. nurture" banner across it on the page that deals with essentialism. "On the question of biology, I have nothing to say," says the speech bubble near Foucault's face.

The book, *Queer: A Graphic History,* explains that Foucault and Judith Butler "never said there was *no* role for biology in our sexuality or gender. They were simply more interested in how sexuality and gender were historically and culturally produced as constructed categories of experience." The section gives a quick rundown of their theories regarding the nature or nurture question, stating that nature isn't a fixed determiner of queerness and neither is nurture. Still, I've always been afraid that people— Grammy, too, obviously—look at me and then look at my mom, look at any of these circumstances, and think, oh, of course.

My version of the scariest book—this book—is that question.

In *Exile and Pride*, writer and activist Eli Clare tracks his own brutal childhood and chews on this chicken-or-egg thing:

"I get afraid that the homophobes are right," he says. "That maybe I live as a transgender butch because he raped me, my mother neglected me. I lose the bigger picture, forget that woven through and around the private and intimate is always public and political."

Clare marks white supremacy, ableism, anti-queer, and anti-transness as abuse in *response* to difference, not as abuse that *caused* the "difference."

I know this doesn't seem like anything, but I'm thinking about teaching. Like, I used to teach *We the Animals* by Justin Torres in intro composition classes and my students were obsessed with the character of the mother, who in the book is a shimmering thing, beat up by circumstance and taking it all anyway. My students would try to write papers proving that she was bipolar or had postpartum. I aimed to turn them from that line of inquiry, their hermeneutics, to poetics. Like, look at the words, what in the book makes you feel like that? What's the form of the thing? What does the writing do? What is it about your subject position that's influencing you? Tell that story, I kept saying. I said it in a certain pulled way and rushed, because it was personal.

What's Grammy reading into my hairs? What does anybody read into any hairs? I think of being read all the time, that mechanism. The root of it is to "put in order," related to *riddle*. (This meaning-making element of the word *read* is unique to English. Most languages instead use a word rooted in the idea of "gathering up.") And I think of the new identity document law in a handful of states that will let nonbinary people identify as nonbinary on their IDs, and how "validating" could be welcome or unwelcome: legibility has ramifications.

Another example:

In "The Pussy Eater" by Carrie Moyer, a glowing, acrylic face is in an ecstatic open-mouthed whimper, her skin is white, she's smeared and bleary, there's a mass of red across her mouth like popsicle but not. The text *Art & Queer Culture* cites the young girl in the painting as presumably covered in menstrual blood.

Apparently, the painting was Moyer's response to the "gay gene" debate in the US in 1989. She was "amused that the emphasis was being placed on locating the origins of homosexuality rather than just accepting it." She was painting against an explanation for queerness, highlighting the absurdity of suggesting a link between the queer body and a bad childhood. In her work, Moyer seems to give her figures agency, rather than depicting them as subjects drawn to women because of some filtered, pathological desire.

"I'm making paintings about girlhood homosexuality, tracking the source of my 'problem' to an imagined collusion between mommy and me," Moyer writes in "Not an Incest Survivor," her artist's statement from 1995 (revised in 2011). As for the entities portrayed in her paintings, she says: "These little man-haters are having sex with each other, eating menstruating pussies, preying on Mother, castrating their Daddies and generally acting up."

But after all the attention garnered for this work, she moved on from making these kinds of images because she got tired of being asked if she was an incest victim.

"Paul McCarthy, Mike Kelley and other male artists who use similar, over-the-top strategies are never called upon to reveal their motivations, much less biographical triggers. Apparently when men use shocking images to depict family dysfunction or subterranean desires, they are addressing universal feelings shared by all," Moyer writes. "However when I employ camp, sarcasm and comparable absurdist tactics, I am 'working through something,' using art as therapy to exorcise demons. The incest reading completely ignores my protagonist: the knowing, rapacious little lesbian who gets what she wants when she wants it."

When I came across Moyer's work in *Art & Queer Culture*, I was struck by "The Pussy Eater" in a kind of delirious way. The youth's face mixed with the blood trips against the frame, and the text that accompanies the image describing her retreat from making this kind of work due to pathologization is even more striking.

Moyer's practice and its reception turn us to unwanted interpretive acts, the force of that on a person.

There's this photo: Mom and me from my sixth birthday. Hank took it. It's black and white. I'm wearing a floral bathing suit and I have nail polish on my thumbs, I've got one arm over the back of a chair, am holding my own hands, smiling in the way I always do, no teeth. Mom's grinning, her glasses are bigger than my face. Our hair is the same shade, mixing, she's leaning toward me. My bowl cut brushes the top of my unibrow.

There's this photo, too: we're at the entrance to Central Park Zoo. Hank is holding my hand that's stuffed into his wool coat, I'm wearing a red beret, a red cape, and am extending a small piece of toast toward a pigeon. He's saying throw it girl, throw it.

I wanted to curl up into a warm sweatshirt of his on the floor. This was his house in Sacramento—orange? The feeling of orange. He and Mom had their second son in that house, the paint cans moved for highchairs, runny carpets.

I liked when Mom and Hank cooked together, held the boys together, put their muscles together, soft and flexed—all four of them, really. The two boys had bodies pockmarked with hand-prints from all the attention—I'd stick my chest out. Hank was Scottish and West Texas Cherokee against white heat. I'd try and pull my hair in a ponytail to match his. I'd measure the color of my skin against his arms, against my brother's legs. I'd roll my pants up.

We'd all be home smelling like sugar and crying off and on and once, I threw a small rubber ball through the window in the upstairs hall, leaving a perfect, round break that I was vaguely proud of. I was looking through the break, it hadn't been fixed, when the bell of a phone clapped around the house. It rang for a full minute drowned out by yelling, a downstairs door slam-ming before falling into silence.

I watched through the break as Hank charged down the street. He juked by, momentum coming from his ass. Mom was draped over his shoulder, her hair bouncing like a sheet, a blonde sheet bouncing. He was holding her butt and running. I watched the configuration of their bodies and the muscles in Hank's legs, run-ning, and at the same time, noticed one of the baby's feet sticking out of the bedroom. He was crawling around, messing with the carpet. He looked at me. A scab on his head moved with him. It was from the day before, from looking for rain. I hit him in the head trying to skip a rock on a puddle. It was an accident.

Sure it was, Hank had said, laughing, one hand in his Levi's. He was barefoot with the ends of his jeans rolled up. The baby was now looking at me, blinking. His hair looked soft in the sunlight, which struck his face, half of his face—our half. I reached out but didn't touch his head, I let my hand suspend there, the sun made a shadow of it that walked across his forehead, he and I watched the shadow together, sinking into the carpet. After a minute, I moved my own hand into my mouth and pretended to eat my fingers. He laughed. I ate my fingers, then grabbed his and pretended to eat them, my lip over my teeth, just gumming.

He and I were still laughing when the sunlight made it to the far wall, laughter suddenly mingled with calls from downstairs, cries. I leaned over the banister to look. Mom's voice traced around the corner.

Come out to the front, she was saying, she was yelling. Mom was in the hallway, calling up to us from a wheelchair, her leg stretched out in a psychedelic way, in a white-green cast.

Hank had his shirt open slightly, he was behind her, peering up, still breathing heavily from running her to the hospital and wheeling her back. He was holding our brother Tye by the hand. I hadn't noticed he was gone. He'd slipped off with them maybe or padded down the sidewalk to meet them. Who was watching? I scratched my leg and looked at them, looked at Gunn sitting in the carpet, waiting for me. The sky was almost pink. No one seemed angry.

Catch some butterflies for me, Mom said, seeing us, motioning her chin toward the front lawn.

I want to sit, she said.

I carried Gunn downstairs, it was rare that I carried him, there was always somebody else doing it or he was operating on his own. I didn't feel like the oldest. He was heavy and smelled like soup.

Hank cupped Mom's elbow and lowered her out of the wheelchair onto the front step, her leg outstretched. He put his arm around her. Mom leaned away from her cast, which lumped there, and put her head on Hank's chest. I looked at him, taut and ruddy—it was an accident, had to be an accident, looked like an accident all over his face.

Go on, Mom said after a few minutes. Go on, so I can watch you play.

My brothers fell off the step, fought on the grass, pretty in their T-shirts, pulling each other's hair, tugging at each other's shorts. They were blonde with round features and enormous eyes. Tye had a bowl cut to match mine, he was three; Gunner, the baby, had hair that stood directly up, his head was shaped like an egg. He'd just turned one, spent most of his time in a chair with wheels and a tray, running. He tipped over a great deal, baby bruises mixed with his hairline. They looked like Hank's boys, exactly like Mom and Hank, a perfect unit, all the same weight and giddy. There were no butterflies. I was six.

Something smelled like sand, my hair maybe, or the light. I couldn't sort my senses out, my insides caught and moved. I watched Tye and Gunner. Mom clapped for them, her torso bounced, anchored only by her leg. I leaned against Hank's arm. His body was cold, almost wet. He patted my leg. I closed my eyes and felt my brother's laugher hit the brick step that was cutting into the backs of my thighs, Hank's body was odd-smelling, forensic. I crossed my arms over my knees, put my head on my knees.

Tye careened toward Mom with a bent clover in his hand. She grabbed him, held him with her whole body. He slipped from her arms and ran back into the yard squealing, churlish, tugging up chunks of grass.

Hank patted me on the leg again with a wet hand.

Mom didn't seem to care. She leaned against that orange/yellow light all cool.

As Mom broke, she became theirs. They broke her, a kind of hazing. I watched it happen. I was huddled close to Mom, we all were. They brought her home.

When everyone was yelling or crying, I liked to stand in this woman's yard, her name was Charmian, and spread my arms out the same width as my legs. I'd make my body like a tent there, or a hanging piece of canvas, would stand at the wide net of her lawn, listen to her TV, picture her alone chewing her nails, her bad halitosis. I'd wear long Little Mermaid T-shirts, no pants, bare feet. The grass was always sweaty, made me have to pee.

Once, toward the end of summer, I was mystified by this silver line of ladies all in black, shuffling their feet on her front walk. I went over to find out what was going on. Mom wasn't around, Hank wasn't. I waded through the grass to get in line and stood with the ladies, like them, except holding myself and jogging my legs back and forth. One woman in front of me turned slowly, her eyes reached over my head, then traced down. She was wearing a black scarf that wasn't wrapped around her throat, it was tied.

Sweetheart, what are you doing? I shrugged.

The woman hoisted me onto her hip, my genitals woke up against the bone. The base of her neck smelled like vinegar and ground beef. She carried me through Charmian's threshold into the darkness of a hallway.

Charmian's cigarette smell was mammoth, there were moth smells, something cooking. The woman set me down in the front hallway and ladies squeezed by. She pushed open a door and shooed me inside, clicked on a light before I had time to say anything: a small porcelain toilet, a wooden lid, a white sink, large mirror. I looked at the woman with my eyebrows raised. Charmian died in the bathtub, honey, she said. The toilet's free. She closed the door. The top of my eyebrows was all I could see in the mirror. I peed.

The woman pushed open the door and gestured at me to wash my hands, the handle was too far, I crushed my chest against the basin trying to reach it. She took me by the wrist and led me out of the bathroom. Her fingernails clicked around my arm. She tugged me outside.

Is this your house, honey? she pointed, Go on home.

She gestured toward my front door and eyed me. I walked slightly away. She stood at the invisible divide between the two yards with her fists on her hips. I paused in the doorframe. My body felt trill.

My little kid self is brave in this text. This bravado is an aspect that doesn't leak too well, it holds in my chest and strikes me as an opening to write this whole thing. In this book, I am somewhere, I realize, my legs exist, my nose does, my face.

There is a tremendous freedom in being the chip of paint peeling off the wall, the one that makes it to the floor.

Mom would give us bowl cuts with a breakfast bowl over our heads, I'd catch pieces of hair in my toes. There were sheets all over the furniture. I don't know why there were sheets. When it was quiet, I'd pick at the skin around my nails. I'd stand behind doors listening for the consonants of my name. Mom would rip at Hank's shirt so that buttons would roll off and toward me.

You're a piece of fucking shit, she'd say, and yank his shirt like she was ringing a bell.

When Hank learned that Charmian died, he struck up a conversation with her family. It was decided that we'd move over there, pay a lot less in rent.

We're moving, Hank had said, taking Mom by the shoulders. She was wiping something yellow off of Gunner's forehead.

Where are we supposed to fucking go, Hank? she said, not looking, her back to him.

Next door, Charmian's, he said, gesturing all around. It's so fucking cheap.

Mom wiped her eye with the back of her hand.

It's the only idea I have, Marie.

You're a piece of fucking shit, she'd say through her front teeth, noise coming from her cheeks.

When boxes started to appear in all the corners, Mom and Hank would go work on Charmian's house and leave me alone to watch the babies. They'd leave me with the one-way monitor and say, if you need anything, just tell us, talk into this, and they'd poke at the plastic. That emergency precaution felt vacuous, like everything else. I'd lay in bed awake and pick at my cuticles. I'd pick them all the way out, lick them. I'd look out the window at the wet-looking spot of old oil stains in the driveway where the car had been before they took it and think about Mom calling Hank "dog meat," I'd play her voice in my head like a song.

When the car got repossessed, Hank was out of town looking for work. I was standing behind Mom looking at this giant red button by our front door that I was told never to touch. I think it was a defunct alarm system from some tenant before us. I was haunted by it, felt forever tempted to touch it. Never did. I loved that car.

Mom had carried me out to it once like that scene between Chiron and

Juan in *Moonlight*—the beach scene, where Juan is holding Chiron in the waves. She set me in the car—a silver Toyota Cressida—I was six. The car smell was thick, fries between the seats. My ear was on Mom's chest, her insides in my head. She put me in the car wrapped in a blanket and the sky looked like a broken screen because it was four-in-the-morning blue. I'd never remembered seeing that kind of blue. She made me the hot chocolate that I loved with the chalk marshmallows already in the packet. I got to hold the hot chocolate myself. It was all of us in the car, but I smiled in the backseat because when we stopped at lights, Mom would put her hand on my knee like, I'm excited to show you something, especially you. We were going to look at hot air balloons. It was some kind of launch in a field near Sacramento. The crash of fire is what I remember.

The man in a gray flight suit handed Mom a car seat from the Cressida that they were about to tow. They could have just driven off with it, he was being nice, he shook his head. She started crying.

Behind us, Gunner was playing with the broken pieces of a board game. He laughed and pushed one of the pieces into his nose. I watched his face contort. He whimpered. I backed away.

Mom didn't look at us when she came inside holding the car seat. She strode into the kitchen and pounded at the yellow wall with an open palm. Her shoulders shook, heart bent toward the floor.

Gunn was screaming.

She pulled the phone off the wall and sat on the floor with her legs widespread.

Gunn's got something up his nose, I said.

She waved me away.

I stood in the doorway and listened for my name.

She didn't look at me, just held the phone like kissing, cupping its receiver closest to her mouth, whispering, looking down.

I listened to Gunner cry. Mom said Jeb twice—Jeb, the guy who had muscles all the way up his neck, hair that traced the whole of his body. He'd come by sometimes wearing incredibly crisp collared shirts, the kind with a white pressed collar and cuffs. He had a little tuft of hair on his head that resembled a small dog, was the top pediatrician at a big hospital nearby.

Mom cupped the phone and then let it hang, it dangled on its cord, twisting, pushing the low dial tone through the house. She wiped her eye with the back of her hand and sat up, hoisted herself off the floor and stood.

He's gonna come over and fix it, okay, guys? She spoke at us, not looking up. Okay, guys? He's going to come help us.

She brushed past us for the stairwell. Gunner's cries were whimpers now against the dial tone. He was sitting up, putting toys into a pile, knocking them over.

When there was a knock on the door, Mom raced downstairs in different clothes, she'd smoothed herself into a blue blouse and tighter, darker jeans. She was barefoot, wiping her nose, red nails raced to the knob.

Jeb and his great wave of shaving cream, the fluorescent scent of faux-rainwater, fought through the door.

Mom hugged him. He hugged her back, left his hand at the small of Mom's back as he did.

They stood in the hallway, their bodies almost touching. Mom pointed toward the driveway, then at Gunn. They stood so close. In one movement, Jeb pulled a thin flashlight out of his front pocket and brushed Mom's hair back from her eyes.

This will just take a second little man, Jeb said, reaching to turn on the light. He kneeled in front of Gunn. Gunn thrashed around. Mom wrapped herself around him, scattering a pastel pile of his toys. The plastic piece fell out before Jeb could do anything. Mom grabbed Jeb's face, kissed him on the side of his cheek, his forehead. They handed the plastic piece to me.

* * *

Hit me, I kept whispering.

No one was listening.

Hit me, I'd say in the mirror or in the dark.

The feeling came from nowhere, really. I would have had it without this childhood, I know that. My hatred for embodiment meant I rubbed my hands red. Did I want to feel or smother feeling? The light in the room was everything.

You know how fruit actually has the fruit fly eggs just on it, really, waiting and ready, and when the fruit starts to rot, that's when the flies burrow inside and eat up, or whatever, and we see them? This ache was like that, always ready, just waiting for decay of some kind to swarm, nobody's fault.

To this day, I watch outward expressions of violence with total remove. The whole time I lived with these people, it was as if I was watching them on film. Something shut off. Before we'd moved to California, I loved New York and I loved my grandmother. My dad lost his job in Dallas when I was two weeks old and we moved in with my grandparents, who were living outside of New York at the time. My mom and dad split when I was eighteen months old, but Mom and I stayed at my grandparents' until Mom met

Hank. They met in New York because Mom was a secretary in his office. When they got together, I was two. They had a huge fight on the turnpike heading into the city and Hank was going to call off the marriage, but then he thought about me, he says, and my little, sad face. They married. We eventually moved to California, myself, Mom, Hank, and their first son, Tye. Gunner was born in Sacramento.

While I was living with her, Grammy would give me 7Up and make baby back ribs and lace cookies and I'd sleep on her couch and watch out the window for deer. The distance that swelled between me and my mother once we moved to California was a grind, Charmian's house smelled like tobacco and rotting lino-leum, drooping awnings and weeds.

Mom frightened me with her body. She loved her body against the air and its childishness, a freedom that felt too intense, too out of control, even when it was light. She'd talk in voices and make noises with unyielding energy—she'd talk to the birds and to the squirrels and had a register of her voice that seemed adult, but was never fixed. She'd flit off into a kind of dream realm easily and fully and we'd do things like cover the car in chocolate jello pudding or let the hose run in the front yard to make mud, she'd roll in it with us and show us how the mud would stick to the white stucco of the house if we raked it with our hands. She made up end-less games, hung donuts from the living room ceiling with push pins and string, had us eat them like that. She made up an entire language, too, it's near unintelligible and difficult to recreate, but it comes from a small part of her throat and fixes words together, there are no Rs and for instance, green crawly became *geencawdie* and means *liʒard*. I was fluent in this way of speaking, I still am.

I watched the movie *Nell* when I was at a friend's in high school and I had a 40 between my legs that I kept tooling with the whole time, I drank it as fast as I could and then spent the rest of the movie picking off its label and trying to drink everyone else's. Jodi Foster was this adult with this voice and was sexual somehow and a child and I'd watch just to the left of the screen so nobody knew I couldn't watch the screen itself. She spent nearly that entire movie in a nightgown shirt dress thing with these eyes that made her so naked. Mom, too, had that texture sometimes and I wanted to fold her into me and make sure she wasn't hurt or threatened and I was hers so it was really only me who could do it. It felt as if we were being tugged toward the center of a sea, not touching. Her body felt like my fate.

This will only take a minute, this will only take a minute, Mom was saying. She was steering, pulling my hand toward her chest, it had slipped, so she was just gripping the fabric, I was wearing a cotton dog costume and she was pulling me down the sidewalk. The crotch of the costume was so low I had to sway my hips to move, had to walk like I was wagging. This was Halloween. I was a dalmatian. Mom's body was so heavy, like the sidewalk. I felt magnetized twice, toward home and away, I wanted to go home and at the same time, I wanted away from everything, her hand. Mom tugged me and I tripped over a woman waiting at a bus stop with several sizable plastic bags and her own children. The two kids I tripped over were dressed as Jasmine. Mom sped us up, she'd seen somebody leaning against the bus stop, somebody whose legs were crossed at the ankles, hanging with muscles and hair. Mom tugged harder toward the body. It was picking at something on its shirt.

It was Jeb.

I found out later that Mom had been seeing Jeb nearly the whole time we'd been at Charmian's. Hank lost his job and was scouting for other jobs in Texas and Jeb would come over and over and they'd started to date.

We're here! Mom said, exaggerating her breathlessness, letting go of my hand.

Remember me? he said, crouching.

I shrugged.

He moved to shake my hand.

When I lifted it, Mom went to hug him and they embraced while I stood there, dangling. I watched their fingers mingle.

The mingling looked red, his hands were red, he was wearing a yellow Hawaiian shirt, gesturing across a small lawn to a white apartment with thin stairs. They walked slightly ahead of me, talking.

Great to see you again, kiddo! he said over his shoulder as we climbed the stairs. There was a fruit bowl of candy by the door, it wasn't full. Help yourself, he said like I was forty.

He moved slowly, swept himself around the kitchen, gesticulated with the wet armpits of his shirt. Mom followed him, grinning.

Look at these, honey-pie, Jeb said. He crouched down and held something into my face. I looked at the hairs on his knuckles that curled over.

It's a model airplane, Jeb said, turning it around.

Mom ignored him.

Why don't you sit here and watch this for a little bit, Mom said to me, spinning toward the kitchen table. She pulled out a chair for me and patted it.

She smelled like heat.

What about trick-or-treating?

Later, she said, and tapped the back of Jeb's chair. I sat down. The vinyl seat squeaked. She took my plastic pumpkin, set it on the table and turned on the TV. I put my cheek on the table, it smelled like old fruit.

Mom and Jeb left for another part of the apartment. Their voices were thin and stretched out against the plaster walls, white carpet, his fat leather sectional. An ice cream truck played pop goes the weasel so slowly outside, the sound like licorice, was loud. A beige-looking woman on TV, flat-faced and staring into the camera, waved her arm. The kitchen lights grew bright against sunset, the outline of a palm tree moved.

I squinted at my own shadow, it moved into nothing on the floor.

I tugged at my collar, my costume, a stain in the dark.

When we moved into Charmian's I was seven and Mom got into the habit of putting me to bed while it was still light out. She'd set me in my bedroom, ask me to change my clothes and get into bed, then close the door.

I'd be awake for hours, gritting my teeth, trapped by the smell of alcohol trailing up the stairs, the sounds of TV growing louder and louder as it got late. I'd think of Charmian, imagine her dead in my bed, her white hair flowing with her smoke. I knew to tell myself that nothing bad was happening. I was very serious about this, *everything is fine*. I'd look all around, try to find something to distract myself with. It was a fairly austere room, I can't remember anything in it besides a bed. I'd rub my feet together under the covers, I'd bite the insides of my cheeks.

Eventually, I learned to press my clitoris until warmth filled my stomach. The warmth would start at my feet, fill my stomach, my face. I'd touch myself to the sharpness behind my eyes, the ugly light.

In an attempt to brighten things, Mom painted my room to look like Barney, a distinct purple and green. She and Hank fought over money for the paint and I told them I loved it even though I didn't. I hated Barney, had no idea what gave the impression that I liked him.

We all hated each other then. Mom hated me, hated Hank. I hated both of them. My hate flashed with longing. Except, all I could picture was more of this, which was also somehow okay.

In 2014, I was trying to write about the Old Griffith Park Zoo, a perfectly abandoned relic, a '60s version of a zoo with huge animal habitats, the whole thing. I started going there to write something, anything, then I got lazy or it got too hot and I stopped. But while I was going there, I'd sit inside the empty, cramped cages that rise up out of ravines, tucked into this expansive urban park, funneled hillside, sagebrush, eucalyptus. I'd close myself entirely in and try to write poems about the plight of animals, but I ended up writing this book.

This story snuck into all of my work for years, embedded itself into my newspaper articles, my wildly unrelated writing, little scenes. This text's first draft was bombastic, there was sex and violence, and I wrote it like that because I always told it like that. I liked the shock. The way it works now though is slow. I'm working with identity like cream, like the smell around someone else's mouth.

While I was first working on this book, I sat in a car with Eileen Myles talking about age-gap relationships.

What's wrong with Mommy? Myles asked.

I couldn't tell if they were joking.

The cultural taboo is so huge! they were saying. It's okay for my girlfriends to call me Daddy, but Mommy? That'd be fucked up. Old men get to fuck boys and girls, they get to fuck everybody, Myles said, gesticulating out the window. Let's try screaming Mommy during our next orgasm, see what that does.

I think of this idea of saying Mommy like *flesh* and the intensity of the word. Linguist Roman Jakobson in his 1962 article "Why 'mama' and 'papa'?" is among those who contributed to this idea that mommy originated from suckling:

"Often the sucking activities of a child are accompanied by a slight nasal murmur, the only phonation which can be produced when the lips are pressed to mother's breast or to the feeding bottle and the mouth full. Later, this phonatory reaction to nursing is reproduced as an anticipatory signal at the mere sight of food and finally as a manifestation of a desire to eat, or more generally, as an expression of discontent and impatient longing for missing food or absent nurser, and any ungranted wish."

When these mouth movements and murmurs are made without anything to suck on nearby, Jakobson thought, they come out as an *m* followed by a vowel sound, and may have eventually led to *mom*. The word holds a breast.

Dad, conversely, was first recorded in English sometime in the 1500s, but its ancestry isn't clear, according to an article on the pop website Mental Floss (a "media company focused on millennials"—full disclosure, I once asked them to write an article about the etymology of *okay* and they did) regarding the origin of *dad*: "even the Oxford English Dictionary throws its hands up."

Who knows though, really? What if *mom* has nothing to do with want? What if it's a kind of hum?

I get that it's not cool to say *Mommy* when we come. I've never been to a fetish fair and seen snapbacks with *Mommy* scrawled across the brim like I see with *Daddy* all the time—not that there aren't a bunch of age play people and other folks out there having a great time with the word, I'm just saying it's not culturally (even queer culturally) as popular. There's something needy about the word Mommy that's maybe too real, like there's an element of power lacking just in saying the name, maybe because of the fleshiness of it. Saying *Mommy* implies that I'm a needy body, I need a body, yours.

In *Kaddish*, Allen Ginsburg is writing of Naomi, his mother, who is made out to have been a mix of insanity and familiarity, he loves her in his description:

"Blessed be you Naomi in Hospitals! ... Blest be your triumph!"

He holds her body up to the light, she's human here, dead and human, after all her hospital stays, his patience, her madness. She entered a psychiatric facility when Ginsburg was in high school, and then for more than fifteen years, she spent her time in mental hospitals receiving electroshock treatments and a lobotomy. He calls her Naomi, not Mom. Ginsburg, in the autobiographical poem, navigates these hospitals at twelve years old, thirteen. When she comes home from one, he's excited, they've prepared for her to return home and play the mandolin again or the piano. He's thirteen. She walks in and immediately isolates herself, disappointing young Ginsburg, who goes to join her in bed:

"'Don't be afraid of me because I'm just coming back home from the mental hospital—I'm your mother—'

Poor love, lost—a fear—I lay there—Said 'I love you Naomi,'— stiff, next to her arm. I would have cried, was this the comfortless lone union?—Nervous, and she got up soon."

Does calling her Naomi save him from the vulnerability connected with saying "mommy" or "mother" even? The poem pushes forward a moment of failed intimacy.

Freud was a champion of sexualizing all kinds of intimacy, positing that everyone is first attracted to their mothers because they are incidentally stimulated by them, girls and boys. But then the boys discover that they have a penis and are fine with it, fine with the idea of pursuing the mother figure sexually. (Freud is here, by the way, harmfully equating gender with genitalia.) Women, according to Freud, though, discover they don't have a penis, they're mutants and lacking, and the mother just reminds the daughter of the lack, so she begins to hate.

"'After the girl has discovered that her genitals are unsatisfactory,' 'her self-love is mortified by the comparison with the boy's far superior equipment.' She is a 'mutilated creature' who, after she 'becomes aware of the wound to her narcissism… develops, like a scar, a sense of inferiority…'" writes the French philosopher Luce Irigaray, quoting Freud in her book *Speculum of the Other Woman*, which deconstructs Freud's essay "Femininity" and a handful of his other writing. She published *Speculum* as her thesis in 1974, essentially coming out against the phallocentricism of the Lacanian community, and she lost her teaching job.

Freud, in his essay "Some Physical Consequences of the Anatomical Distinction Between the Sexes," published in 1925, suggests that people with clitorises should stop touching themselves like that: "The reactions of human individuals of both sexes are of course made up of masculine and feminine traits. But it appeared to me nevertheless as though masturbation, at all events of the clitoris, is a masculine activity and that the elimination of clitoridal sexuality is a necessary precondition for the development of femininity."

Freud argues that when masturbation isn't working, because the person with the clit is dissatisfied, they have to put their wish for a penis aside and replace it with their wish for their own child, which hopefully brings a penis along. All this time, they're mad at their mom for their genitals, for "sending them into the world so insufficiently equipped."

Recently, I had a meeting with a PhD student at a coffee shop on Sunset in LA to talk about trans autobiography as a diagnostic tool—that's their work. They're studying early gender clinics from the '60s and '70s and their framework around understanding trans. The centers would regularly use this technique in which a patient wrote out their story, an autobiography, essentially, and the clinicians would analyze it for diagnosis, not totally unlike what my students were doing with the mom in *We the Animals*.

This PhD student was knee-deep in boxes of research from Robert J. Stoller, a psychiatrist who started the UCLA Gender Identity Clinic in the 1950s. Stoller was a psychologist who specialized in gender and was famous for advocating psychological "treatment" for trans patients and discouraging surgery. This could be seen as bad, the student was telling me, but unlike so many of the clinics who did surgeries on people and then sent them off into the world to be stealth—disappearing into the fold and passing as a cis person—this guy was spending time with non-passing trans people for decades.

This is what came of all that time: according to this research, Stoller posited that trans people are trans from being smothered by hyper attentive moms. Michigan University researchers apparently countered him and argued that "high" and "moderate" classifications of transgender people resulted from different causes. (My assumption here is that these classifications, high, moderate, etc., are coming from Harry Benjamin's Sexual Orientation Scale, which was based on Kinsey's scale and gave points based on people's desire for reassignment surgeries or body alterations in general. You'd get a six, for example, if surgery was an "urgent" want.) Michigan argued that transsexual people classified as "high" had been influenced by too much mom, and those classified as "moderate" by too little mom, an indifferent mom. It's always the mom that gets the blame, the student said, eye rolling.

"As for the role of the mother in transness…" they emailed me after our meeting, prefacing an attached document from a box that Stoller had labeled "Too much mother."

The document, written by Stoller, read: "By the time he was a year old, this boy's gender needs already mirrored those his mother unconsciously wished upon him: his transvestism was caused primarily by his mother's wishes."

The emphasis belongs to the PhD student.

In Irigaray's 1979 text *Et l'une ne bouge pas sans l'autre,* she asks a generalized mom figure to do something about all this, to release her. The piece is a performance. Like, fix the feelings of inadequacy somehow. Like, why can't you? She attempts to show the pain of being a mother and a daughter in a masculine paradigm.

"And the one doesn't stir without the other. But we do not move together," Irigaray writes. "When the one of us comes into the world, the other goes underground. When the one carries life, the other dies. And what I wanted from you, Mother, was this: that in giving me life, you still remain alive."

If I am my mother's wishes, who am I anyway? How do we get out of this? Get rid of the mom, says psychoanalysis. In theory, Stoller's suggestion for avoiding "too much mom" may have been to just get out of the scene, excommunicate Mom from the mind, become autonomous.

I was at a pizza shop the other day that had a person—SCOTT was printed on his T-shirt in big block letters—making balloon animals in the take-out section. I was waiting for my food, watching. The balloon guy had a large board with images on it that kids could choose from. It was hard though because the images looked like temporary tattoos (realist cartoons in full color) but balloons don't look like that and a lot seemed to be getting lost. A kid pointed at a picture of a guitar and both Scott and the person with the kid—the mom?—ignored them. How about Thor's hammer? the mom-person asked. The kid pointed back at the guitar. Oh, you know, we've got a great robot, Scott said, pointing at the high-contrast photo of a robot. Do you want that? The kid looked near tears, their nose turned red, they scuffed the ground. What do you want? the mom was asking. The kid pointed then at this Minecraft character thing that was a green blob. Oh honey, don't pick for your brother, pick for you! she said. The kid's body jolted against this idea. They turned away from both of the adults because they were starting to cry. All the kid's limbs looked weak. The mom squatted down for a hug and eventually, the two picked an alien together and I left while the balloon guy was trying to convince the kid it was the alien from *Toy Story* hanging by a claw.

Why couldn't the kid just get the guitar?

You have to choose for yourself, take care of yourself, is something I've heard. My grandma likes to say I'm good-natured, that I'd do anything for anybody else, and that I have to learn to do more for me. But do I have to shove everyone—Mom, particularly—out of my mind to get there? What if there is no such thing as a place of pure "me"?

"As [the philosopher Julia] Kristeva famously puts it, 'For man and for woman the loss of the mother is a biological and psychical necessity, the first step on the way to becoming autonomous. Matricide is our vital necessity, the *sine qua non* of our individuation,'" writes Maggie Nelson in *The Art of Cruelty*. Nelson asks us to "note that the subject here imagined [by Kristeva] doesn't simply outgrow or separate from the mother. It murders her."

If you look up matricide on Wikipedia, they also give a long list of other -cides, including avunculicide, the killing of one's uncle, and nepoticide, the killing of one's nephew. And on the page, there's a painting by William-Adolphe Bouguereau from 1862, which is known as *The Remorse of Orestes* or *Orestes Pursued by the Furies*. In it, a muscly guy has his genitals obscured by a sheet that's twisted around his arm, he has his hands over his ears and seems to be running away from a clot of femmes. One has been stabbed with a dagger and is reeling back, a red cloth draped similarly over her arm and streaming from her hair. Another femme has a torch, they're all reaching toward the dagger in the woman's breast. The man seems to be escaping. He's killed his mother to avenge his father's death and it looks like he doesn't want to think about it. He flees.

Nelson says that she doesn't know why matricide has to be the sine qua non of our individuation and questions violence as a route to individuation. But nonetheless, she says, along with our desire for separation—and the inherent guilt that accompanies that desire—comes "the question 'What have I done? Am I a criminal?'"

I am guilty of needing a body, a mother's body or someone else's. I am guilty of imagining what other people would want when I think about me. I do feel guilty when I bar my mother or my brothers from my thought process, like the balloon kid was told to do. I feel guilty when I give myself over to me, whatever that is.

Right now, I'm sitting here with my lips pursed around an imaginary nipple. I'm looking out the window and trying to make "mom" in that sucking way. It's totally easy. I'm just pushing sound out with my lips in a pucker shape and it does sound like I'm calling. Maybe the word did come from there, the sound of sucking or missing out on sucking. It's also possible the guy made it up.

The boys were sitting in a small tent in Charmian's yard they'd made out of a tarp, they were covered in ketchup. I waved goodbye to them. Hank was saying, wave at your sister. They looked at me and held their elbows up. Hank kept his eyes at the tops of their heads, warm and sweaty, held his mouth near their ears. Mom had her hand looped around my bicep and was pulling me toward Jeb's car. She'd been talking about Jeb's car for weeks. *It's not* repossessed, she'd say, humming *essed*, clicking her nails together. We're leaving, she'd say, pressing me, hugging me before bed, this leaving is all we've ever wanted, remember?

I believed her that we wanted it because her eyes and her body were convincing, her hands were warm, she'd whisper about not saying anything to anybody. I wouldn't because who would I tell?

Now this was it, and the boys waved and kept waving. I didn't. I froze. Mom was tugging me into the car, the leather was weedy, smoke was weedy. I felt kaleidoscopic, like I was being held at an odd angle.

When the car doors closed, Jeb passed Mom his cigarette and she held it to her mouth, turned to me in the backseat, smiled with the cigarette.

You ready to go to our new house, baby?

Her voice was tinny, she'd found a new octave, was using it to activate a new baby-sexy way of talking. I watched the boys waving as we pulled off the block. My palms sweat. I had to pee, I said. They weren't listening to me.

The plan was to stay at Jeb's apartment while he divorced his wife. I slept on a futon pressed against the refrigerator for a month before the move. We were supposed to be going to a permanent house.

When do I go back to school? I asked.

Mom was stepping over the futon on her way to the fridge. She was bleary and in a robe.

When we get to the new house, she said, pulling out a can of diet coke. She looked off and at the countertop, opened the can of coke without looking at me. Cold moved up my body.

That night, when she and Jeb were both out, I emptied all the cupboards and tore into a bag of brown sugar, poured it into my mouth until nothing else rushed, just me.

When we moved out of Jeb's apartment, I did get the nice kind of pressed-board bunkbed like I'd always wanted, a blue area rug with boats. I slept on the bottom bunk, looked up at the ceiling, drew an ampersand on it with my face. In this new house, I'd gotten into the habit of putting myself to bed. I didn't brush my teeth because I didn't have to. I never shut my door, theirs was always shut.

We're going on a trip tomorrow, honey, Mom said, tousling my hair. She checked herself in the mirrored wall of the living room, sipped an auburn drink. An ashtray steamed next to her. Jeb walked from their bedroom shirtless, dragging his cologne.

They fell into each other's faces.

When I woke up the next morning, Mom and Jeb were gone. No one was home besides me and the dog. They got me a dog. I named her Rose for no reason, she was a yellow lab puppy that shat and pissed.

The house had a hot tub in the center of its courtyard, an entire mirrored wall, two bedrooms, one bathroom, a garage with Jeb's model airplanes, his windsurfing gear.

I crushed across the carpet, paused in a sunspot on the floor.

Rose was rubbing her face near little puddles of her own shit.

I loved the dog, didn't want her to get in trouble, so I scraped at the poop with the broom and dustpan. I took loads of poop through the living room to the kitchen trash can on a drippy pan, then set the dustpan and the broom on the kitchen counter and emptied out half the cupboards to look for a bag of sugar. I tipped over the cup of sugar packets next to the coffee maker, ripped open four and poured them into my mouth.

Jeb was the kind of guy who cared about carpet. I'd catch him on all fours, pulling particles out, putting them in his nose, or with the bead of his finger, into his teeth. He'd brush the sides of his nose, brush the sides of his head, brush his pant legs, brush his chest hair, turn red, charge around the house looking for something, keys or something, talk about the '49ers.

I got my first detention that year because I poured a line of purple Pixie Stix out on my desk. I looked at it for a second, pushed one side of my nose closed, and leaned in. My classmates scooted away from me at their desks. Purple sugar poured painfully from my nose for the next twenty-four hours.

The doorbell rang.

It ping-ponged through the house. I wiped my hair from my eyes and looked at the door. Maybe this was Mom. I looked around at the mess I'd made. I tried to straighten it, put the ripped sugar packets in the trash, wiped my hands on the front of my pants. They forgot their keys. They're being funny. I walked to the door.

I opened it. There was a smiling woman on the step, she was in a lime-green shirt and jeans. Her hair was lumped on top of her head. I came up to her stomach. She put her hands on her knees and bent forward, you're supposed to go with me, she said.

I watched her finger. She moved it through the air toward our driveway, where a silver minivan had pulled up and parked. Its driver honked and waved.

Where's your stuff, baby? she asked.

What stuff?

She pushed past me into the house, motioned toward the person in the car. She saw the dog and its shit, the shit-coated dustpan on the kitchen counter, brought her hands to her face.

She walked into the kitchen, grabbed a plastic grocery bag out of one of the cupboards, went into my room and put a pile of my clothes into the grocery sack, handed it to me.

Fifteen minutes later, I was in the third row of seats in her minivan. Something smelled like pee. The kids, three of them in the second row, were older, all speaking Spanish, smiling at me.

We pulled into a parking space. Multicolored tubes loomed over the concrete ahead. Somebody put a towel around my neck, grabbed for my hand.

The waterpark was small, had a few tubes, yellowed pink slides.

I ended up on a ladder. There was air between my legs and my ass like I'd never felt it. Someone was counting to three.

I was dragging my hands through a thin trickle of water at the mouth of an enclosed black plastic tube. I caught the feeling of my body on the edge of something—the feeling, its heat, was new. I wanted to stay there, stuck somewhere, but somebody else pushed me off. I bumped down the slide to a bend. There was supposed to be a little trickle of water down the middle, but it was dry. My skin streaked against the dry plastic and burnt. I skidded to a stop, still high up, stuck.

Minutes passed. I sat inside the tube and watched my own stomach extend from breathing. I figured I should conserve my breathing. I crossed my legs and heard something hitting, a thud, a body, I braced for it. Another kid, its legs bowed and shining, pushed us into a shock light, the break of a pool.

I splashed up, gasping, pulling the hair out of my eyes.

I couldn't find the family, ended up wandering around until it was dark and the park was almost closed, listening to filtered water leave and enter all the tubes. An attendant said my name over the loudspeaker for a long time before the woman found my hand at a kiosk.

I still have no idea who these people were.

Just now, looking out the window as I write, I saw a puppy take a shit on the end of its leash. Its owner was tugging it along, not realizing it had to shit and was shitting, the dog tugged back but the owner never noticed, and now there's a new turd out on the front walk. The dog was scolded for walking slowly and got tugged along, the poop fell between its legs.

I want you to know that this waterslide and this experience was exciting and menacing and I slipped freely from everyone into the pool.

But then fear crept in. I grew up knowing fear as an inheritance of femininity.

Apparently, my great-great-grandmother was too scared to leave the house and would only talk to people through the mail slot. Inside, she'd crochet replicas of the house, perfect ones with trees and holes for the windows and a swinging door. I always pictured these replicas in cheap pink yarn but I don't know what color she used. My grandma said she'd display them in the windows—fractals kind of—and that's all anyone saw when they looked in. She died falling down the stairs. My grandmother talks about her mother's fear of everything— storms, strangers, hard candy. And my grandma talks like this, too, before we hang up the phone she regularly cautions me not to fall in a hole. I've been educated in this fear, a contrast to all the stories about men in the family, who adventured into the navy or to faraway jobs.

The "feminine," writes Irigaray, is only allowed and even "obliged to return in such oppositions as: be/*become*, have/*not have* sex (organ), phallic/*nonphallic*, penis/*clitoris* or else penis/*vagina*, plus/*minus*, clearly represented/*dark continent*, logos/*silence* or idle chatter, desire for the mother/*desire to be the mother*, etc..."

This line from Irigaray comes from *Speculum*. She's using Freud's language—he famously called womanhood a "dark continent"—and goes on to say that femininity is "unfathomable and unapproachable; its nature can only be misunderstood by those who continue to regard women in masculine terms." She posits that femininity, or the symbolic system that holds femininity as an opposition to masculinity, was made up by men. Thinkers, many trans thinkers, disagree with Irigaray's use of the body and the basic framework of essentialism she uses to talk about being a woman, often grounding an experience of woman-ness in genitals. She uses the image of two lips and mucus in her essay "When Our Lips Speak Together," for example, to make her points about femininity.

Still, this is what I'm wondering: if "femininity," as Irigaray uses it, is only defined in opposition to the masculine (via masculine terms) is there something somewhere else? Could "femininity" instead be a stand-in for something other than non-masculine, something outside? I want to be the slash in all of those examples. Can I?

What if my access point to this question is my mother's body? All twisted up like me.

I'm writing about motherhood.

When I am my mother's child, am I also myself? In my mind, I face her with a slight bend to my knees. I am focused and strong. I don't know how long I can hold the position.

I do wonder how much of myself comes from holding like this.

I recently listened to a lecture by Catherine Malabou about Lacan and his symbolic phallus. When Lacan uses the term *phallus*, he's not referring to the organ, but all that the penis represents: power, dominance, ability, etc. He's using it as a symbol, thinking about how we speak. Like when we say cock and really mean power.

Lacan proposes this: in all of language, we have the word or the sound and then the meaning (the signifier and the signified—he's getting this from Ferdinand de Saussure), like *dog* in English is accompanied by the idea of the animal that's different from *cat* in a handful of ways. Mostly, we all agree. Lacan is saying there's a gap between the signifier and the signified, it's imperfect. Actually, he's a little more emphatic, he says that words destroy the thing they represent, "the symbol manifests itself first of all as the murder of the thing."

There's a gap between the words and their associations, there's a gap between *cat* and the meaning of the word. We've all generally agreed on what these words signify, but there's always something missing. This, says Lacan, is what allows us to project. You can project yourself onto me because of this linguistic thing. Because of this gap in language, there's a gap in me.

It's kind of like that game people played in middle school, that thought experiment about colors, like what if my "blue," or the color I see when I say blue, is really, for you, the color you see and call red? And we'll never know! The words are separate from these agreed-upon meanings, they float there. Like, can you describe blue? It's beautiful and is the color of the sea. Right, but someone's hue might be entirely different and still function the same. Do you see what I mean? Another example: I know the meaning of the word trans will change in my lifetime, it's inevitable. I'm waiting for the word to signify something I can't comprehend.

In her lecture, Malabou was saying, if the phallocentric economy is symbolic, and basically symbolic of dominance or power, how do we get out of it? I think all the time about what ways I can have power without being part of this economy, she said, and I haven't found a way out. We who occupy gender (all of us, probably) are without our consent being projected onto. If I show up in the world as "woman," what is projected onto me is "lack," if I show up in the world as "man," what is projected onto me is the phallus and all the power associated with that. But none of these qualities are actually essential to any gender, or any genitalia, anything!

I appreciate Lacan's idea of the phallus as a symbol in our imaginary that results in vast effects. Malabou explained that she herself is hyper aware of every time she acts as the phallus, which even as a cis woman she can do. She can act in the imagined phallocentric way, wield what we imagine as power, predicated on someone else's "lack." But she doesn't want this to be the system. Speech is symbolic, so even talking about this reaffirms the paradigm—the language we use (here, English) is phallocentric to begin with, not to mention colonialist and violent in all sorts of other ways. What else do we do?

I hang on the idea of appearance.

These days, I like to swim. I'm still freaked out by water parks, but I swim regularly at the public pool nearby and sometimes when I'm there with a friend, somebody will say to them, Oh that's nice you're here with your son today. I always just end up trying to say something sarcastic and then I swim laps knowing I need more tattoos. It's not that I look so masculine, equally as often, somebody's like, oh, where's your shirt young lady? My hips hop over the waist of the tight swimmers' shorts I wear, my butt sticks out—attributes associated with femininity, I guess. Most often, I feel like those plastic Rubik's Cubes for toddlers (maybe no one else remembers this toy, but I had one) where if all three layers of it are lined up, the toy makes a fireman, a nurse, and a dog, but you can scramble them. Know what I mean? You can have a fireman face and a nurse middle with the legs of a dog.

Recently, I was watching a talk by the artist Pilar Gallego who created this character named Mouth-Head. In the piece *A Spectacle*, which Gallego produced in 2014, Mouth-Head wears navy swim trunks with white spots and is lying on a red-and-white striped towel. Gallego refers to Mouth-Head's outfit as a superhero costume, the character itself is made of Poly-fil, insulation foam, wire mesh, papier-mâché, thread, cardboard, acrylic, liquid latex, broom bristles, and has a breathing-simulation apparatus. It's life-size. Mouth-Head's chest bumps up and down like breathing, it puffs their brown belly and chiseled abs. The whole head is just this mouth, permanently pursed, red lips and teeth. For this installation, Gallego made a beach scene by filling the floor of a CalArts gallery with sand. They and a friend (a cis gay guy) then lay in the sand alongside Mouth-Head. They jostled their legs back and forth, rolled onto their sides, looked up like they were in the sun.

Gallego said the point of Mouth-Head was to play with a body as illegible, to reclaim "ugly" as a term, to juxtapose their own self-described "curvy" body and their friend's "boxy" cis-male one. The beach scene served as the site of exposure and was a nod to Riis, a queer beach in New York. Gallego wonders if they can move "woman" or "man" off a body, peel back the signification. Mouth-Head was meant to thwart unwanted interpretation. What is the body that can't be read? Gallego asks.

The idea of freedom is important here too.

In his book, *Black on Both Sides*, C. Riley Snorton juxtaposes Christine Jorgensen's famed transition in the '40s with the lives of six Black trans folks who were also in the media at the time for their transitions, to a much different effect. None of their lives became emblematic of an American individualist freedom to be oneself that Jorgensen came to symbolize, particularly because validity as a trans person was already determined by "passing" and surgical transition, which was hard to access for anyone who wasn't white and middle/upper class.

Snorton quotes Emily Skidmore in arguing that Jorgensen "was instrumental to the construction of the 'good transsexual,' whereby she and other white trans women 'were able to articulate... the norms of white womanhood, most notably domesticity, respectability, and heterosexuality.'" Snorton goes on to say that "the Jorgensen story was instrumentalized into a narrative about personal triumph..."

This "personal triumph" part is important.

A striking story in Snorton's text is that of James McHarris/Annie Lee Grant (as they are referred to by Snorton) and the images of their chest binder published alongside an article in *Ebony*. The caption describes the binder as a "homemade band of white cloth," calling it a "gimmick which helped [Annie Lee] to fool thousands."

The article pitches the idea that "Something... happened to her long before she started wearing men's clothing only." Snorton suggests that the writing invokes "sexual violence as a possible catalyst for McHarris/Grant's 'change'" and crafts an argument about their "deceitfulness." Unlike Jorgensen, McHarris/Grant is labeled as traumatized into their gender, as if they possess no agency surrounding it, zero "triumph."

I think of Mouth-Head and the point of Gallego's work, intended to address the projection (racially, sexually, and gender-wise) of others onto a body. Gallego suggests: okay, so this is how my body is interpreted, but what if there's a disconnect? What if there's actually nothing about me that's singular? Who has the power to decide?

A lot of these books, recent trans ones particularly, are about agency and becoming. Right now, there's a list of thirteen or so trans autobiographies on Amazon, part of their "Best in Transgender" list, and so many either have "becoming" in the title or hint at it. Part of the root of the word is "possession," in this case, self-possession, which is like to own, but I don't get it. I have no handle on myself.

I wonder if unwanted interpretation is a symptom of the case that Irigaray lays out, the masculine paradigm, in which there's a closed loop of white (European-descended) maleness that actually names itself everywhere and is the thing against which all other identities are defined.

Irigaray ends her essay with this quote of Freud's:

"That is all I had to say to you about femininity. It is certainly incomplete and fragmentary and does not always sound friendly..."

Recently, I watched a grainy video by some guy who'd hooked a stingray on his fishing line. He was dangling the stingray above a dock on his line, tugging at it, toying with it. Halfway through the clip, its body started shuddering. He didn't let it go. The stingray fought and then grew still. Its mouth was opening, opening. A slit grew across its pelvis, grew to gaping. It shuddered some more, one small diamond shape crawled out, then another, then four. Babies fell from inside the stingray onto the dock, flapping, squeaking, wrecking themselves trying to get at her. The guy with the fishing line held her suspended, shaking her body, shaking the line, laughing.

I watched the video by accident because of auto-play on Facebook. I deleted the app.

Once, I watched Jeb hold Mom against the living room bookshelf by her neck and she turned a kind of purple I'd never seen. He shoved his hand down the front of her pants with all the muscles of his back, looked like he was hammering. She twisted, twisted like a chicken, her mouth open.

When Jeb released her, Mom crumpled to the floor.

She tried to crawl to me, crawled with her hands splayed out, her shoulders up to her ears, her mouth was chapped. I ran.

When we had to run away from him, Jeb would find Mom in the dark like a mouth. We moved from hotel room to hotel room until Mom pulled my curled hand out of hers and put it into a flight attendant's. I wore a plastic necklace with some kind of identification brochure slotted into it, fingered that plastic necklace while I rode on the plane.

Once, we ordered pizza to one of those hotel rooms and I had to hide with it in the closet because Jeb was coming, he'd called Mom from the lobby or the parking lot of UNO's or something. Mom told me that I broke her heart because she could hear me inside the closet, singing a lullaby she'd written for me. I do remember moving my finger through the slats of the perforated sliding door, singing:

Oh the moon / and the stars and the wind in the sky / all night long / sing a lullaby / while down in the ocean / so dark and so deep / the silvery waves / rock the fishes to sleep.

On our last night in Jeb's house in Sacramento, I was staring at Mom's mouth, she was yelling from outside my first-floor window. Her mouth was curling up and down, she looked left and right, wrung her hands. She wanted me to jump, was pounding at my window.

I watched her beating the screen, my name was coming out, hitting the window, bouncing into the lawn, the palm trees. Her eyes were moving all around.

I moved slowly to influence how fast she was going, to make everything slow. I padded out of bed, stepped on each boat on the carpet, she banged harder behind me. I didn't look back, I pulled open my door.

Jeb's body, blood trickling down his leg, blocked the doorway. He was naked aside from maroon boxers and was in the hallway, the hallway just outside my door, yelling at no one, just the wall, slamming our white corded phone into its holder. Sweaty chunks of broken phone shot crazy into the carpet. I watched his face contort, fast and slow, revving.

I bolted out from around Jeb's legs and ran into the front yard, stunned by my own mix of horror and adrenaline, yoked to a level of satisfaction that seemed like crescendo.

Mom was outside, holding herself by the shoulders. She was topless, her breasts wagged against a light fog. She held herself and a smatter of wire glasses that he'd broken over her nose.

I watched her standing there, her breasts framed against the dark, beating on the lawn.

A black sedan pulled down our street, moving so slowly that its tires seemed to push the concrete away. The sedan pulled into the driveway. Two men got out. One of the men, shaped like a refrigerator, put his suitcoat around Mom, then held the car door open for us both. Mom scooted into the backseat. She was six years old, I was seven or eight. We drove for a few minutes in silence before he said I'm sorry this happened, Marie.

She shivered and shrugged.

Too much of her was showing, so much skin, the men looked at her. I watched out the window.

I didn't find out until adulthood that the man who came to pick us up was Jeb's lawyer. We never went back.

When we pulled up to his house, the lawyer's wife helped us in, Mom smiled. His wife's box braids brushed a long housecoat. She and Mom held each other around the back as she walked Mom to the bedroom.

I asked for a glass of water.

The lawyer blinked at me when I asked.

Over here, honey, he said, walking me down the hall.

Two kids with fresh faded haircuts peeked out of a room that he walked me past, they looked surprised.

When I walked into the bedroom with my water, Mom was already turned toward the wall, sleeping maybe. There was only one bed, a big king with a wrinkled duvet, two digital clocks that flashed on either side, a sliding glass door that led to a grassy backyard and an elaborate set of playground equipment. I lay awake watching a yellow flag on the playground equipment shake.

Writing, I am aware of the raised hairs on my upper and lower arm like my body has a fever: a mentor of mine who read this book's first draft called it trauma porn, she had the preceding part circled in red.

By porn, I'd like to think she meant I emphasized sensuousness.

My mom can write beautiful things and she had the foresight to write me a lullaby about the sea which is my most favorite thing. She knew me enough. I like that idea. She also taught me to read, said that I was reading so early and part of it was because she'd make this caterpillar thing where each book I read was recorded on a plate-sized circle of construction paper and taped to the walls around the house. She enforced reading time, would make the house stop for an hour or so for reading, and I'd lay under a table and love my own attention. I am grateful to her and her genius, her love that looked like this.

I won't forget Jeb beating her. I won't forget how much heat there was coming from the house. I have never forgotten rolling the sleep out of the corners of my eyes, glancing over at Mom: her body wagged and was wounded, it wound me up.

This responsibility was monstrous and is still glowing, a porn.

This is the site of Mom's raw body and Jeb. I decided long ago that what happens to women is what happened to her. A gap. I didn't invent it. Now, I push myself to look at the body and its mechanics like a vacant lot, to know the parts and relate.

II.

My grandparents were blinking down the runway.
I was eight years old. They stood side by side
with their arms behind their backs, shifting
their weight. Grandpa was tall with a crop of
curled hair, Grammy was swarthy and short, with black curls, big
rounded features, warm tan skin, eyes. She was always wearing
short-sleeved polos, my grandfather, too, they matched vaguely.

The first thing I said was, I remember you.

Where they lived in New London, off Long Island Sound, they
had a gigantic white anchor and a beach, craggy beach all around,

a lighthouse visible a few yards away—two lighthouses. The sky was gray, the lighthouse beam was bouncing off the clouds. In the distance was a plant, a smoking, steaming Pfizer plant and a shipyard, large masts extended through the fog, schooners, a cluster of submarines, sparks flying from a welder.

There were cold stone steps that led up to a porch on the second floor, a brick garden, a small cove, a knocker on the front door, a rock in the basement to keep the house from falling into the sea, a WWII bunker because of the naval base—I'd play down there when I got restless, close the gigantic iron door on myself and look out of the tiny bunker window onto the lawn.

I ran my hand along everything, broke away from my grandparents and ran up to the second floor, ran down the carpeted corridor, ran back downstairs. I toed a compass etched into the wood on the floor of the kitchen, the cream-colored wood used for north was worn and low.

This is a sea captain's house, Grandpa said, standing with his hands in his pockets. He had a mechanical chess set next to his chair, a little magnetic chess board with red lights that lit up to indicate where the computer moves, and you move the pieces there yourself. He played after dinner, wore two flannels at a time, kept every penny he's ever found. To this day, if I visit his house with nothing to do, he has me put change into rolls.

This is you, he said, and tapped his finger on a frame.

Two photos hung on the wall beside the kitchen. One was clearly of him inside the cockpit of a boat, he had a pipe in his mouth and a sou'wester on his head. Below that photo was one of a little girl with her hands on the sides of her face, she was wearing a small straw hat and a sweater, wasn't looking at the camera but at a pile of leaves being blown up into the air. There were no other photos on the walls, just big paintings of ships.

Your grandmother took these, he said.

She looked back at us and nodded.

When Grandpa was old enough for college, he left Ohio for the Navy. He'd grown up in an apartment with his mother and a sister. None of this went well, apparently, sounds like he spent a great deal of time in the closet while his mother was out. He was little in a dark closet, picking at his shoes. I've never met his sister, I don't remember meeting either of my grandparents' families. Grandpa became the husband to my grandmother, who I love so earnestly, a kind of love that's brassy and sometimes cold. I warmed Grammy by accident. She loved me more than anything and her love for me surprised everyone.

As I got to know her, I learned that Grammy smelled just like warm leather, like the interior of her Volvo, or the sweetness of baby powder mixed with her Volvo. I learned that if I went with her on errands, she'd buy me sherbet, buy me pairs of blue-black overalls that I'd wear shirtless around the house.

I'd stand in the weirdly feminine mirror of my weirdly feminine room—I say weirdly because neither of my grandparents tended toward rigorous gender roles, but this was a sort of altar to the possibilities of femininity: pink ruffles on everything, an expressionless doll in an antique stroller. I would stand there and love the feeling of the snap-metal catching against my nipples.

Who is gorgeous? Who can hear me?

That summer, I read *The True Confessions of Charlotte Doyle* about a girl on a clipper ship who became one of the crew, lived in the forecastle and was called Mister Doyle by the end. Doyle climbed the ratlines. I scaled the bannister.

Grammy bought me a fisherman's cap that I refused to take off, a black one with thin ribbing that matched my overalls. There was nothing I wanted more than for my nakedness underneath clothes to match the movement of the sea, the light on my walls from the lighthouse next door, the lighthouse—a kind of joy that hadn't cracked for me ever. I curled toward the sun.

During those first few weeks, my grandparents sent me to a party with some other kids from the block. It was supposed to be a costume party, I wore my Charlotte Doyle outfit, a yellow pillowcase that I'd cut up and then sewn with some thick yarn so it could be a shirt/dress. I added a few patches for effect. I called it my sack cloth, wore it constantly. All the other kids were Power Rangers. There's something separate about me, I told Grammy when I got home.

In the evenings, I'd slip out from my bedroom with a belt around my stomach that I'd tucked my notebook through. I'd have two pencils tucked into the belt and would slide down the stairs on my stomach. The light of my grandparents' TV would arc toward and up the stairs. I'd get caught in the glow, moving. At the base of the stairs, I'd brush my hair behind my ears and take my notebook out. I'd crawl on my elbows, weave across the wooden floor behind the furniture, pausing under tables to hold my breath and write. My grandparents would look at one another, push their TV trays away and cross their arms over their chests. A gust would rush at the windows. The metal of my overalls would drag along the floor, I'd wince at the noise and hang there, perched and perfect, describing in detail the backs of my grandparents' necks.

Isn't she gorgeous, Grammy said. Look at the light on her face. That's not just pretty, that's a beautiful woman—Ingrid Bergman, she wanted me to study Ingrid Bergman's symmetry, her eyelashes, her lips.

Each afternoon before we watched a movie, Grammy would sit with me on the rocks back-to-back. Her back was warm and she was mostly laughing, our toes would swing toward the sea. My body would purse for lightning, thunder, fat rain. In the heavy breeze, her short black curls would lift, my bowl cut would be flat and behind my ears. The stack houses and smoke pipes would groan at the mouth of the sound, foaming white against bruise-black rain. She'd listen to me so intently. I'd explain to her what I knew of each different cloud formation. I told her about cumulus congestus, warned about hail. She let me talk nonstop and play expert, happy and whole.

Grammy ranked women in two categories, pretty and beautiful at varying degrees. Ingrid Bergman was top, Grace Kelly was just under that. This was my experience of the sea: Grammy's resolute attention. Grandpa was busy working and she and I were left alone to feel what it felt like to be similar, something happened between us as sameness, identity as same.

When Mom moved in, she would always try to be near Grammy and me. She'd call at us, waving. I'd wish she wasn't there, tugging at us, trying to play, but she would open the car door and hold it open with her knee.

Hey honey! she'd say, want to come with Mom?

Go ahead along with your mom, Grammy would say, we've been sitting here all day, she would move to get up.

I'd hesitate, then I'd look at Mom's face, expectant, soft, and I'd feel a surge of urgency, a subtle rising guilt. I'd slide off the rock toward her.

Mom arrived at Grammy's after bottoming out with Jeb. I was there for several months before she joined us. I don't know what happened at the bottom. She's never said.

When Mom walked off the plane in New York, she was wearing an all-white tennis outfit and carrying a racket. Her smell dragged into the terminal, floral with a sharp pinch of acid. She and her mother hugged, she hugged her father, too, then me, but lightly, still looking up at them.

Everyone's voice raised in excitement. I fell into the background, blended in with the patterns of people, patterns in the carpet that seemed to charge out of the airport.

She's been such a good girl! Grammy said, reaching back for my hand and pulling me next to her.

Good, Mom said, linking arms with Grandpa and leading him away.

As the airport fanned out, Grandpa went off ahead with the luggage. Mom reached for my hand, but Grammy'd grabbed it. The cool of Mom's hand brushed mine and she pulled away, she hugged her tennis racket.

There was a kind of competition between us that ran through with comradeship. I'd fallen into a sort of superior kind of love that was separate from codependence. It was light. Still, I'd feel an overwhelming guilt, more acutely now that Mom was there, but always, really, for doing the things I'd begun to love, like writing at night, crawling behind all the furniture, taking a notebook out to the sea, loving my mother so much that it looked angry.

Mom would much rather that I cry into the backs of couches or with my ribs running against stairways. When she'd get me in the car, she'd whisper to me about God or something, then take me to a church that was on the same block as my school. The chapel was shadowed with heavy white marble floors, bloody Jesus. By the door, there was a softened wooden pedestal with a cube of laminated cards, the twelve disciples pictured on them.

I didn't know what happened to her while we were apart or why she was so invested in church, but she'd walk us quickly to the altar, shoes crunching grit-red carpet. She'd wipe her hands on her apron, then move the thin of her legs into kneeling. She was working at the Seaman's Inn, got the job waitressing a few weeks after she moved to town. She worked all night, had to wear a black dress with a white apron and a white doily in her hair. I liked to finger the doily when she laid it on her dresser, paper like lace. In the church, her apron would fold into her knees, and I would set my backpack down by her and kneel with her because that's what she wanted. I'd watch sunlight from the stained glass zip through us like rosy, hot water—I don't think her parents ever knew we did this.

After a few minutes in the church, she'd reach into her pocket for a dollar. She'd hand it to me and motion to a wooden box full of candles on our left. I'd slide the dollar in and we'd light candles for no one I knew, I almost always had to pee, would sit on my foot and push my pelvis into my sneaker.

Once, I was wearing a new quilted blue coat that I was supposed to keep clean, I rubbed the side of my foot against my crotch. I rocked. I held my breath. I rocked. She drove us away from the church toward home so slowly. There was a mother and her baby walking in the road. I clenched my fists at my sides. Mom was talking. Her voice knocked around the car. I pictured running up the stairs to the bathroom, kept picturing it. I was working so hard. I couldn't. I didn't want to. I peed.

I soaked my foot with the most confusing warmth, peed all over myself with the weight of a nine-year-old, the needles in my stomach fanned out. I wondered how to hide it. My coat caught a great deal of the pee, some slipped down the seat and onto the floor. I was afraid to move. Mom was lost in a glassy somewhere, I was wet.

Not long after this, I came home from school to find a doll with a green body, sock face, and red hair in my chair by the window. "I made you this honey," Mom had written on a little note tied to one of the doll's wrists, "I know things have been hard." I brought the note and the doll with me the night she took me to an apartment above the pizza place in town. The apartment belonged to a guy I'd never met. He'd waved at us from the street and lifted off his heels a little in a young way as he did. He was smiling, he left us alone as we walked inside. There was a cardboard advent calendar with most of the dates punched out sitting on the counter and a clock shaped like a banana on a strip of wall above the sink. The apartment smelled like sea, Mom moved around like it was hers. She pulled out a black shoebox from a cupboard in the guy's kitchen. I made all of these for you too, she said, passing it to me. She sat down in a kitchen chair while I opened it and put her chin in her hand. Her face looked taut, tired. There were ten or so dresses for the doll in the box Mom handed me. The dresses were sewn with minuscule stitches from some of my old T-shirts, my favorite one about herbs with drawings of lavender. Mom'd sewn every dress with a red button where the doll's heart would go. The whole thing was secret. I kept the doll in my desk at school until the newness wore off.

In the evenings, Mom would wait by the phone for hours. There was a desk chair and a rotary phone on a table by the kitchen. She would wait to talk to the boys in Dallas, to Tye and Gunn after school, at six o'clock. They were six and four years old then. Her hands were always in her lap. Grammy'd keep asking if she was hungry. Mom would smile, say no.

If I ran past her, she'd pinch the outsides of my cheeks with her thumb and forefinger and say you can't be like that. You can't make this harder. So, I'd walk quietly around the house, would cross my legs, use only pencil because markers run.

Why's your hair like that? I'd ask Grammy, leaning against the arm of her chair while she curled her thick black hair with a hot iron, sitting on the porch.

Gypsy, she'd say, misunderstanding.

I always thought she was Hawaiian for no reason, I knew she liked Hawai'i. I'd draw pictures of her with brown crayons and coconuts. I didn't know what I was doing. She'd tell me that she came from a place like Ohio and left all that family, and Gypsies just keep on moving.

I won't ever move, I'd say and she'd get quiet or tell me about a fireball that once fell through the chimney and shot through the screen door, left a basketball-sized hole, sizzling, while she was a girl eating peach ice cream on the porch.

I felt for my stomach when she talked about it, the hole in the screen door, burnt lightning like me.

Come on out here and see this, Grammy said, handing me a greenish thing. She reached under the cellophane and fondled a light green jumper, scrunched her face. Like a Brillo pad, she said.

I touched it with her. I scrunched my face. I wore it for Mom when she got home from work. She was standing in the mirror, she had put a temporary rose tattoo onto her chest. I watched her skin, watched the rose crinkle as she lifted and lowered her arms.

When she first moved to New London, Mom would let me cuddle her in bed, just for a few minutes before I left for my own room. I always wanted to hold her face. She'd shoo me away if I got too close. Mom was pinning something into her hair and when she turned to glance at me standing behind her in the mirror, there was a pin still in her mouth.

It's my uniform, I said.

I watched her face, her face wasn't moving.

Grammy is feeding you too much, she said.

I looked at the skin around my stomach. I pulled at it. I picked at my face. Grammy would make me a milkshake every night and we'd eat popcorn all day.

I began to try countering the milkshakes by jogging up the stairs. I'd come home from school and run up and down. Grammy asked me what I was doing and I told her I was trying to get skinny. She laughed for a while, then put her hands on her knees. Don't listen to her, she said, her face dropping. Her coarse collar brushed my check.

During parent-teacher conferences, Ms. Kelack told Mom that she thought I was retarded. The kids wrote my name and the chubby boy's name on the board with a heart around it. No one talked to me at lunch or anytime. I wrote in my notebook about the hems of their uniforms, their hair. I brought my notebook out to the parking lot that doubled as our playground. I sat on the curb and described each of my classmate's facial expressions.

Dear You, I wrote, it's today.

Grammy kept saying, don't worry about all of them, don't worry about them at all.

I started getting headaches.

You are my champ, Grammy would say, putting a bag of frozen peas on my head.

Mom got headaches too. We all did. It's a genetic thing impacting all our joints, cervical spine most seriously. A little blue light pokes at the periphery of my vision as a warning that I've been upright too long, it's my head cutting off blood vessels to my brain. (Yvie Oddly the drag queen has it, was talking about its impact on her life in episodes of *RuPaul's Drag Race* in Season 11, pulling neck skin out to show how stretchy it is, hurting often. I've never known anyone outside my family with it, so it's been nice to point to Yvie as a way to explain.)

I wrote a poem about pain.

I wrote three poems about pain.

I turned them into one poem about clouds.

I copied the poem down and submitted it in the box on Ms. Kelack's desk and weeks later found a glow-in-the-dark rosary on my desk with a sticky note on it that said first place in pencil.

I stared at the rosary, brought it up to Ms. Kelack.

Is this supposed to be for me?

She moved papers around on her desk and nodded.

Wait, I won? I was yelling.

It seems that way, dear, doesn't it? she said.

During the assembly, I put my poem onto the wooden podium and walked over to the microphone, popped it off of its little stand and paced around like a televangelist.

This is my cloud poem, I said.

The audience laughed.

My grandparents fidgeted with cups of tea in the front row. Mom missed it because of work. I wore something red, a red print dress.

When the old man officiating things called my name I listened for the last syllable to tip out of his mouth, waited a beat before standing, smoothing out my dress, and walking over to the podium. Light bounced off the knees of everyone looking at me. I heard my steps against the tile, felt my hands around the microphone, the blood in my body was loud.

Everyone was smiling. When I was done, I put the mic on the podium, strode off the stage. I sat in the metal chair next to Grammy and she held me around the shoulders—that was the best one, kiddo. She said it over and over into the top of my head, that was the best one.

They took me for sherbet and we sat in the car. Grandpa parked pointed down a hill so we could see the water. Grammy elbowed him, I told you, I told you she's going to do alright. We watched the lights on the sound shake into fog, brilliant lights doubled on the water. I sat in the backseat drinking up the car smells. We drove home like that, I cradled my tiny plaque.

When we pulled into the driveway, I shot from the car through the front door, calling for Mom. My grandparents glanced at one another and followed me up the stairs. Mom was standing at the top of the stairs holding the phone.

I've got a job! I've got a job! she said, rising to her toes. I've got a job!

She grabbed me, shook me by the shoulders.

We're moving!

This is a photo I have: we are wearing jeans and crying. My hands are in my pockets and a marble notebook is under my arm. There's ocean, dust.

We were heavy, leaving for Dallas to be with the boys.

My grandparents stood with us in the driveway. Grammy was heaving with emotion, her body hulked against the wind, her lips were pulled, sequined.

None of me wanted to leave. I jerked from their hugs hot and afraid.

Mom had her arm around me and pulled me to the car. I was waving, awkward.

Nothing will be as good as this, will it? I had asked Grammy before bed on one of our last nights.

She and I were watching a movie together, it had Gene Kelly in it. I was supposed to have been asleep hours earlier but Mom was waitressing. Gene Kelly was swinging on an absurd velvet curtain.

I don't want to go, I said.

She didn't respond, just mixed food together in one big kind of bowl, moving slow.

* * *

Those first few months in Dallas, we stayed in Hank's apartment on Abbot, which had two cats, gray carpeting, cupboards full of beef jerky and football memorabilia. Somebody would smoke cigars near the carport. Mom would put on *Emeril* and make Tye and Gunn whip cream mounds that they'd put their faces in. They'd watch cartoons all day, she'd pee with the door open.

I slept on the top bunk. My brothers shared the bottom, Mom slept in Hank's bed and he slept on the couch. I'd carry my notebook into the carport overhang and write stories while it hailed, would stand behind Tye and Gunner while they played video games on a small TV by the window. Their heads never moved, the carpet was too sweet. I wanted to call Grammy every day but it was long distance and I had to wait until the weekend. They were watching *ThunderCats* and *Jurassic Park* and other things I hadn't heard of. On Saturdays, I'd sit on the low bookshelf near the bathroom and call Grammy.

She'd say how is it and I'd look around at the boys playing on the carpet with some new remote-control thing, Hank was always gone. I'd look out the window at the concrete, at my own toes.

I hate it, I'd say.

Oh, it'll be okay when you start school.

No it won't.

She'd pause.

Call me anytime, she'd say, it's going to be okay. But if it's not, I want you to call me. You promise?

I promise, I'd say.

She'd cough like she was crying.

I teeter on this proposition: Texas. The white women were small and blonde and drinking and the white boys were thick and sunned and chewing, they all looked strong.

Mom opened a cupboard in the closet of her new classroom and pulled down a box filled with Ball jars. She pulled out one of the Ball jars and held it by the lid. I put my finger on the glass. A wet lizard lolled around inside.

It's in alcohol, she said, angling the jar so the lizard moved. The lizard looked dusty even though it was wet. She found the box in a back cupboard of her classroom when she moved in.

Go ahead and look through it if you want, she said, and left for the teacher's lounge and coffee.

I picked the jars out—two seahorses, a mole, pinkish noses pressed against the glass.

The room was sizable with a row of windows on one end, leaf green carpeting. Mom had been decorating it for days, had created little stations with area rugs and rocking chairs and all the things she'd made, perfect things, something called a "warm fuzzy" and a "cold prickly," if you were good, you got a neon-colored cotton ball with googly eyes glued to it; bad, you got a Styrofoam ball stuck with toothpicks. She had a "soft friend"-making station (was always opposed to the term "stuffed animal," it seemed too violent, and so invented "soft friend") and a reading area, with bookshelves arranged to create intimacy, a standing lamp she'd brought from home, large animal-shaped pillows that she'd sewn, strewn across the floor.

The kids weren't there yet. No one was.

I watched Mom move through the space with scissors and laminate, pushing her glasses onto the bridge of her nose. She smiled so extremely.

Got your helper here with your today? José, the third-grade teacher, called out from down the hall. He was on his way out.

Yes, a big help! Mom called back, smiling, glancing over at me.

Droplets of rain knuckled leaves just outside the window, afternoon light softened toward a storm, exit signs in the hallway grew bright. My reflection in her glasses was lit by Mom's face, an arching row of clouds.

Everything I ever knew about my mother and my relationship to her was rooted in phallocentricity.

Despite anything good, I saw her lacking. I saw her trying so hard to become the thing someone wanted to possess. I treated her like she didn't know anything and wasn't capable. Like when I was starting to drive, I'd never really been behind the wheel and was shaky and lost. I felt too dyslexic, I confused left and right. I couldn't afford a car either, so it was kind of irrelevant and I gave up for a while. I was frustrated when it was my brothers' turn and both of them took to driving fast and without issue. I'd forgotten that by the time they'd started driving both of my brothers had had little matchbox cars in both hands for forever and had driven go-karts and cars, too, occasionally. I didn't realize that lifelong training toward agency contributed to their ability. I internalized this kind of thing and pushed it at Mom. I didn't respect her, stripped her of "Mom" or "my mom" as a title. I'd call her Marie. She's never liked her name.

Butler has a new lecture out about monolingualism and gender, the idea that gender as we understand it in the West is coming through the funnel of English, which changes everything. As understandings of gender become more expansive, she argues, we have to account for the language.

"We should seek to bring about a world that is more livable for the many relations to gender that exist, the many languages for gender, and the many ways of doing or living a gendered reality," Butler says in her 2017 lecture given at the European Graduate School.

Irigaray's argument is angled this way, too, though she's focused on the importance of recognizing that these languages (romance languages specifically) are patriarchal from the start. How do we talk about our mothers, how do we think about our mothers with a new language?

"We also need to find, rediscover, invent the words, the sentences that speak of the most ancient and most current relationship we know—the relationship to the mother's body, to our body—sentences that translate the bond between our body, her body, the body of our daughter," Irigaray writes in *Speculum of the Other Woman*. "We need to discover a language that is not a substitute for the experience of corps-à-corps as the paternal language seeks to be… clothing it in words that do not erase the body but speak the body…"

This is the truth: I want femininity to be roomier. More enormous.

Gender like a tub, not anybody else's so much anymore. But maybe there's no real escape.

We moved to a duplex in Dallas that had a front gate, a yellowing cube of lawn, it was next to a water tower that had its own plot of grass and a driveway around back. This was after Hank's. There was wall-to-wall white carpeting. It was a railroad with trailer-park sized windows, a small kitchen with a built-in bar.

Gays probably owned this, Mom said to Hank when we moved in, pointing at the leopard-print wallpaper and the ornate ocher faucet in the bathroom.

One night a week the boys were supposed to stay over, there were always wrapped boxes of new video games on the seats of their favorite chairs. Mom swept herself up around them, swung through the house opening all the blinds. She'd wear a long jean dress with a sweatshirt over it, speak with a slight lilt, like a child, crushing across the white carpet.

Popcorn, do you want popcorn? M&Ms? Pizza? she'd coo. Tye and Gunner would pop their headphones out to hear her. Nah, they'd say in unison.

Do you want to get dinner together? Take a walk? Watch a movie? We can do anything you want, she'd say with her hands open.

Their faces would make no movement. She'd spend herself on them anyway. And after hours of cajoling, Hank would pull his truck into the driveway and idle there. The boys would pick up their bags and hurl themselves out the door. I'd watch Mom wave at them out the window. Her back seemed small, slipping. The duplex was dark except for the sheen of idling screens and the level whirr of highway. She'd turn away from waving and we'd look at each other. Her face would flash with longing and I'd imagine that she might fold into me, sobbing. But she'd turn away. She'd hug herself and she'd rock.

In the mornings before school that first year in Dallas, I wore humongous plastic gloves and learned to say "all y'all," put my backpack in a closet in the kitchen and fit on a hairnet. I was always alone in a freezer with dry, acrid meat, looking for something huge wrapped in plastic, chicken-fried steak.

The cafeteria had a neon sign shaped like a star and these expensive-seeming tables with little blue stools that flipped out of them. I started working there in exchange for free lunch because I was alone in the cafeteria for hours in the mornings. Mom would drop me off early on her way to work. I didn't tell her what I was doing.

In class, my hands were always cold from the frozen cookies and trays. The other kids thought I was insane. I didn't care. All the ladies shook like Grammy, laughing. I'd go outside with them on our break before the breakfast service. They'd smoke Virginia Slims in this weird little courtyard and we'd look at each other's feet.

You should go back in there, they'd say, go hang out with the other kids, they'd gesture with their cigarettes.

They don't like me, I'd say.

How come? They'd all coo, scratching heads through their hair nets, elastic cutting.

Because I'm new and I hang out with you guys, I'd say. I was alone and wasn't trying.

They'd nod. We'd watch each car as it pulled up to the stop sign on the corner opposite the townhouses. Breaking, moving. Breaking, moving. The lights of a 7-Eleven up the block made the grass look more neon.

The trees shake like napkins, I said.

Everybody nodded some more.

I forget sometimes that one of my classmates that whole year paid me a nickel a day to carry her lunch tray around the cafeteria for her while she loaded it. I'd bring it back to her table then leave to go sit by myself.

I started wanting cigarettes. We were all alone with our want.

This is what *woman* meant, Mom told me, not having anything and having to work for everyone forever. We came from a long line of domestics or housekeepers. We were wives and widows and women who worked from the neck down.

I was unattractive, I had purple stretch marks on my hips and my chest where my body was pulling apart, where the weight had collected then sloughed off. I had one hair on my pubic bone and bad, heavy bangs.

I'd stare into the mirror before Mom got home from work, touch the breasts that were ripping themselves into mounds, fill my hands with them, purple and hanging.

I pulled a pair of scissors out of the drawer and leaned over the TV to get a good look at myself in the mirrored wall behind it. Jerry Springer was on. He was yelling something like, Which one of these ladies is really a man?! The audience was roaring back in hyperbolic horror.

I listened and looked at myself, my cheeks were too round, my bangs were childish. I put the scissors to my temple, snipped at the bangs on the right side, a hunk of hair fell into the white carpet, a breeze moved the plastic blinds, smelled like jasmine.

I kept snipping. I went along the right side of my head so that I had stubble almost. I tried to mow it down, make it the same length. When I stood back, Mom was a dark mass in my reflection. I hadn't heard her come in. When she saw me, her bag dropped from her shoulder, my hair falling all around.

Even now, I look prepubescent. I'm hairy everywhere except my chest. These purple marks are now strands like white mucus running, sunburst. I remember that year trying to tug a hair across my lips, out of my vulva, like a stray strand, and finding it was stuck.

When I cut my hair I was in a sort of fever. I wasn't trying to be manly, but there was a nightmare in my chest about how I looked and how I was being seen.

Freud does so much with the trope of the masculine woman, he writes about how she is desirous of the penis and is stuck in the stage when she was a little man (during prepubescence)—he describes this as part of the preoedipal stage where the woman discovers her clit, and is learning of her lack.

Irigaray refutes this by arguing that Freud's only point of reference for the confusing world of womanhood and women's sexuality is the (symbolic) penis and more penis.

Honestly, I just wanted the bangs gone.

Now, I question my choice to leave my chin hairs scraggly and long, little black loops like holding hands.

In 2011, I was naked aside from a chest-less green gown in a Canadian cosmetic surgery office located on the second floor of a mall on the outskirts of Toronto. This man was cupping my breast and swirling it all around, he was going to cut it off, along with the other one, in a few hours. The doctor held my boob through a blue latex glove, moved the fat of it around as if he were a claw gripping a plush thing in an arcade machine. He drew a fat black line across my skin where my breast usually lay.

I'd just signed the form that said "paid: $6,043.00/ male reconstructed chest" and was slowly realizing that these were my last few moments with breasts. I was so busy getting the money together that I hadn't taken any time. Five thousand of it came from a settlement after I got hit by a car crossing the street in New York—you got lucky, my friends said about the money and I agreed. For now, healthcare can cover top surgery, it didn't then. I realized I hadn't said goodbye to my potential to give milk, any of it. Cold in this man's hand, they were beautiful. Historically, they were the most complimented parts of my body, aureoles dark as my grandmother's face, a gift from her that I was supposed to empty into a baby's mouth.

I looked at myself in the mirror over the doctor's shoulder. My brow was wrinkled, my frame seemed so small. He let my breast fall and stood up from his stooped position. It lumped there. I looked down at it.

Look okay? he asked.

From a part of my throat that was surprisingly high, I said great, it looks great. I tried to imagine the lines as scars. I tried to imagine how I'd look with big hips and no breasts, a subtracted pinup, some gasp.

A number of my friends had gone to the more famous doctors (Brownstein, Garramone) in the US. I'd decided on this one because he was one of a very few who didn't require a letter from a psychologist, didn't require a written promise from me for a full "physical transition" either. In 2011, the US wasn't interested in having a bunch of us in-between and running around. They didn't want us going halfway anywhere. So, to Canada!

A few years after I had surgery, I was at the $20-for-an-entire-day spa in Los Angeles's Koreatown and a woman who'd been eyeing me for the better part of an hour cornered me to ask if mine was the same surgery that Angelina Jolie had.

The best I could do that moment was "sure."

You were afraid you'd get cancer?

Sure, I said again.

You're so young! You don't want to get implants? She pulled at her own nipples in gesticulation.

Nope, I said.

Weird, she responded, then lay back down on the wooden sauna bench, put her towel over her eyes.

Naked, I look like Pan, a satyr or something, I still have hips, little legs, I'm hairy with a thin waist, a slight chest, chewing gum nipples, broad shoulders. I'm so small. I've edited my body, mixed my skin around with some money.

Now, twisted, puckered scars serrate my chest and sometimes strange women on the beach cup me by the elbow and say, Sweetheart, just because you have cancer doesn't mean you can walk around like this. They mean, it's still obscene for you to be topless even though the lumps of them have been tossed out into a biohazard bag in some fluorescent Toronto storeroom, even though after surgery, your boobs became singular—a chest.

I remember a therapist once, a counselor, talking to me off the record about a couple she called "the interesting couple." They were once lesbians, but one member of the couple was coming out as trans and they were in therapy trying to deal with that and the frustration of seeing themselves possibly as heterosexual, as queer, as something other than lesbian.

The therapist was giddy about using dysphoria as the diagnosis and giddy about telling me:

Apparently, gender dysphoria is "a difference between one's experienced/expressed gender and assigned gender, and significant distress or problems functioning." It has to last at least six months.

"Until the early 1990s, when trans communities began finding strong, collective voices, medical providers' explicit goal for gender transition was to create normal heterosexual men and women who never again identified as trans, gender-nonconforming, gay, lesbian, or bi," writes Eli Clare in *Brilliant Imperfection.* "Transition as an open door, transness as defect to fix, gender dysphoria as disability, transgender identities as nonpathologized body-mind difference—all these various realities exist at the same time, each with its own relationship to cure and the medical-industrial complex."

Diagnosis is from the Greek *diagignoskein*, which means a discerning, distinguishing. The root dia- means "apart."

In sixth grade, I was put into special ed and it was clear that the whole point was to separate kids like me out. The intention seemed to be to move us into a category of unskilled workers. I don't know if there's a correlation between my attempt to buzz my head with those scissors and this placement. We had alternative math classes that were about adding and subtracting groceries or things from a hardware store. Their job was to create productive, efficient, docile citizens. The ones who weren't cowed killed themselves, two kids did from my group. A friend of mine hung himself off his bunk bed by his dad's tie.

The history of categorization around disability in the United States was always about social control.

I was happily diagnosed in many ways because it removed me from having to perform like other students, which I felt totally incapable of doing, but it also ensured my separation. There's something wholly destructive about how our access to medical services is predicated on docility and productivity, which relies on this separate-ness to function.

"Rather than diagnosis, I want us to reach toward our own familiar, ordinary bodies and histories: Explain to me your hands resting still as water before they dance. That I cannot imagine," writes Eli Clare of his own hands and his experience of cerebral palsy.

This idea of familiarity versus normalcy is perfect to me.

According to the American Psychiatric Association, the whole point of developing a system to classify mental illness was aimed at collecting statistical data. And the first attempt at getting this data was in the 1840 census, which recorded the rates of "idiocy/insanity." The APA cites that by the 1880 census, seven categories of mental health had been determined: mania, melancholia, monomania, paresis, dementia, dipsomania, and epilepsy.

"Viewed over history, mental health symptoms begin to look less like immutable biological facts and more like a kind of language," writes Ethan Watters in *Pacific Standard Magazine* about the Diagnostic and Statistical Manual of Mental Disorders (DSM-V). "Healers have theories about how the mind functions and then discover the symptoms that conform to those theories. Because patients usually seek help when they are in need of guidance about the workings of their minds, they are uniquely susceptible to being influenced by the psychiatric certainties of the moment. There is really no getting around this dynamic.... The human unconscious is adept at speaking the language of distress that will be understood."

I appreciate what Jasbir Puar writes about the link between the trans body and the disabled body. She, too, brings up the DSM-V and writes about its shift from gender identity disorder (GID) to gender dysphoria.

In 2012, the American Psychiatric Association's board of trustees approved changes to the DSM that took out "Gender Identity Disorder," the general diagnosis for transgender people, and added "Gender Dysphoria," which now diagnoses *symptoms* of gender incongruence and not the identity of transgender itself.

Puar argues against this, suggesting that just because some trans people want to move away from the idea of "disorder," that shouldn't mean others who need medical care should have more difficulty accessing it, which is what she posits this DSM shift will cause.

Clare's work in *Brilliant Imperfection* hangs on this nexus. He's writing against cure. Accosted by people regularly offering cures for cerebral palsy, he argues that there's no inherent need for him to cure it. The cure model is faulty. There's nothing "wrong" with his body, it's inaccessibility and ableism that are wrong. He applies this logic to his trans-ness, is he trying to "cure" it by receiving hormone treatments and having surgery? Why does he refute the need for surgical treatments for cerebral palsy but embrace the changes that are afforded him through gender reassignment?

"I could have turned my desire into a diagnosis, named it gender identity disorder, declaring myself a man who needed a man's body-mind, and surgery a cure. But my yearning was more paradoxical than that, as is the body-mind rightness I feel now, never missing for one instant the weight, size, shape, or sensation of my breasts," Clare writes. "I need that messier story because there is no real way to reconcile my lifelong struggle to love my disabled self exactly as it is with my use of medical technology to reshape my gendered and sexed body-mind. I can either try to fix the contradictions or embrace them."

All these years, I've held onto this giant red folder of my special education paperwork, hundreds of loose yellow sheets with signatures of ladies I don't remember who'd been assigned to me. My mom started the folder when I was in sixth grade and eventually gave it to me. It's got my test results, report cards, yards of observation notes, and it's astounding to me that I exist as this paperwork, the pages I have are all copies, the school kept the originals, probably got rid of them by now, but I'm in these lists that say my strengths are listening to directions and my drawbacks are listlessness and unresponsiveness to visual cues.

I was so excited by this diagnosis. I cried when they called and said I'd scored so low on the Wechsler Intelligence Scale for Children that there was no way they could keep me from special ed. I cried and Mom thought it was because I was upset and I smiled at her through the crying because I was so relieved. There's no paperwork anywhere with any exact name for what was up. They don't know what it is. I just failed the test badly enough and that led to my relief.

Similarly, I used to wish I could tell people that I had a chromosomal difference. It would get me out of this anxiety about pathology if it could be explained through physiological diagnosis, I figured. I remember getting tested for my testosterone at the clinic when I'd dropped off a friend and I was really really hoping it would reveal that I'm just genetically different, with a higher amount or something. But our hormone levels change all day long and things don't just work like that. I didn't get any substantiation. Now, I realize there's nothing to make sense of. *I can either try to fix the contradictions or embrace them.*

Here's another one: Maybe there is no way for a symbolic regime to be ethical, my friend Brandon said when he read this—we worried together about new nonbinary or gender neutral categories, that there will just become a trinary, or a second binary (binary vs. nonbinary), and nobody will get free.

I was talking about this recently with the poet Jos Charles, who referenced Eve Kosofsky Sedgwick's suggestion that we lack criticality when we opt for new binaries in place of the old ones. "For instance, a binary of one versus the infinite pervades the idea of infinite genders, the normative vs. non-normative, which can at times let people off the hook," Jos said, referencing Sedgwick's *Touching Feeling*.

"Somehow it's hard to hold on to the concept of eight or thirteen (and yet not infinite) *different kinds of*—of anything important," Sedgwick wrote.

Jos is suggesting that sometimes saying, Well, there's an infinite number of genders! can actually function as dismissive and also make for this new opposition: there's a "normal" gender and then a forever's worth of other combinations.

In *Undoing Gender*, Butler writes that "[t]here are advantages to remaining less than intelligible, if intelligibility is understood as that which is produced as a consequence of recognition according to prevailing social norms."

Inevitably, any set gender unintelligibility will become symbolic of something eventually, grabbed and subsumed.

I don't have a ton of hope that it's possible to get out of this economy in any larger way than just moment-to-moment interactions.

I watch this thrashing sometimes inside myself, I realize, a worn masochism.

When the doctor left, I flipped through *OUT* magazines giggling, a nurse put an IV in my arm. There was a stream of nurses in the office for the next half hour until one of them said everything was ready and encouraged me to follow her.

I was jolted by her sweetness. I'd been working at stoicism, tried to rein in my feelings as I walked into the operating room on my own power.

Is this how cosmetic surgery always goes? The scene was nightmarish. Awake and elective, I hoisted myself onto an operating table and lay there. I was surrounded by several people in head-to-toe scrubs, cleaning implements, scalpels, things. They moved without looking at me. A fluorescent light beat.

When I woke up hours later, a nurse was shaking me awake. She was saying it's time to get up and was struggling to put a brace around my chest to keep the newly reconstructed skin in place. I welcomed the feeling of the brace, my body was a loose glove. She handed me a juice box, apple, I think, and shooed me off the bed and into a wheelchair.

I sipped on my juice box and felt heavy in the canvas cup of the wheelchair.

Three weeks after I had surgery, I sat on the toilet where the light was best and opened the brace on my chest. I had to have a friend take my stitches out because a drive back to Canada for a fifteen-minute procedure seemed absurd, and there was no nurse or doctor in the area that had any idea about top surgery. I was living rurally and was scared of the repercussions of going into a doctor's office with this new thing. My friend stood there with the scissors as if with a wand, snipped away the first blood-soaked sponge from my new nipple. I almost threw up from the feeling. It wasn't pain so much as a weird, sensitive numbness that felt like stomach lining, tugged.

They peeled the sponge back to reveal a tiny crater and winced, seeing it. They squinted and picked with a pair of tweezers at the tiny striped stitches—tons of them knit into my crushed new nipples.

Their wince was gorgeous.

In the counseling office in middle school, a heavy-faced woman with a cat-shaped doorstop asked me about my bangs, asked me to turn to the side so she could see them, asked me about my period, too, patted my hand. She talked about her period and hormones and her husband. She passed me a Tootsie Roll while she was talking. Her head seemed huge.

She pulled out a folder with my name on it, then tore a pinkish note from a pad and scribbled.

Go to this room and tell them I sent you, she said.

Mom had called them, she was freaked out by my hair, had them pull me out of class to go to the counselor, sent me a cookie bouquet.

The person who pulled me out of class gave me a pass to the counselor and the bouquet, several purple cookies shaped like bears stuck into a foam piece in a basket. The card said, "I love you honey, I'm just worried." I rubbed my thumb across the note, looked at how Mom had looped the "l." My body careened around. She loves me, was my thinking, she actually does.

I carried my cookie bouquet around with me while I looked for the second room through a maze of poorly lit hallways, pushed open a door and gave another woman my note, there was a din of thin paper—so many papers the sight seemed like a noise, pastel sheets everywhere.

An older woman in a large flowing skirt and an enormous red belt led me to a windowless room with a small table lamp and two cushioned chairs, a brown area rug.

She sat me down in one of those chairs and told me that I was about to take a test, that the test would last for five days, we'd meet every day in this room.

When she asked me if I wanted something to drink, I said coffee.

She was warm, squinted at me when I said it and told me to hold on while she looked for some. She went to the teacher's lounge and brought me black coffee in a Dixie cup.

I took her test.

I had to put together pictures of fruit and dissect a poem by William Blake—I didn't have trouble because I didn't try, I wasn't asked to study, so I didn't.

Did they decide if you're retarded yet? the cafeteria ladies asked every day during the test. We're just checking on you, they'd say and push me on the shoulder and laugh. Don't worry, all of us think you're perfect, they'd gesture in a circle at all of the kitchen appliances.

I'd talk to Brandy Vasquez by the curb every day while we waited for the DART Bus. I brought my sack cloth from Grammy's to show her once, Brandy sat in the grass and watched me do a monologue in a fake British accent about clipper ships. When I was done, she stood up and gave me a sort of kind pat.

Brandy invited me on a sleepover. It was Friday. Mom didn't answer when I asked if I could go. She got out a Tupperware filled with dolls, Barbies, a bunch of tiny accoutrements (hairbrushes, houses) and dumped them out on the carpet in front of the TV. She bounced into the carpet with them. Her eyes were big and blue.

We can have our own sleepover! she said, wagging my doll—I'd chosen it once when Mom wanted to buy me one on a random trip to Target, I picked out a femme-dude army nurse in an apron. He had plastic hair and an infirmary cot.

We don't need anybody else, she said, crossing her legs on the carpet, brushing her doll's hair. We're a team.

I watched her in the mirror, had gotten into the habit of looking at her though the mirrored wall of our living room rather than into her face. Her eyes were turned down, she scared me. I was with her, low and underwater.

I found a photo of Mom and me from that night in some box at my grandparents'. It's a bad out-of-focus photo, we're standing in the mirror in Mom's bathroom, I'm holding the little stick that's used to color somebody's hair, her hair, she's got foils in and is making a wild party face like it's spring break. We both look a little drunk.

The thing is, I hadn't noticed anything was wrong exactly. I knew she was sort of dating someone and wasn't talking to me about it, just coming home smelling like cologne. She was distant.

I'd just raced home to tell her about school, I was a freshman in high school and I had gotten onto the newspaper staff, was one of only seven kids that did out of like twenty or something, which felt important. I'd just gotten off the bus, always got off two stops earlier than I was supposed to because once the bus driver told me I had beautiful eyes and not to tell my parents. Nobody else lived off the highway, I got made fun of regularly for having that address—hwy as the full thing. So I'd get off with the kid that lived on one of the last normal streets and run.

When I pushed open the door of the duplex, there was a burning smell, soft smoke, an alarm chirping. I looked around, smoke curdled around the edges of the windows in the half-lit house. I held myself as I wandered around, needing the bathroom but calling for Mom. Something was burning. My cheeks thudded.

A pan was sizzling in the kitchen. I could hear it. A pool of curled cinnamon was stuck brown to the bottom of a pot on the stove—incense. I turned off the stove and waved at the smoke, crushed across the white carpet.

I squinted through the house—went toward the bathroom.

In the hallway, Mom's hand was open and empty. She was naked and prone, her hand splayed out like a body.

I put my backpack on the floor by her hand and knelt down. One nipple from her small breast pushed from under her, her glasses were still on. I put my hand on her back, felt for her breathing. Laminated alphabet cards for her class were spread out at the end of her bed. She'd come home early or something. The room smelled like alcohol. She was breathing.

I pulled out the pair of thin pajama pants with the roses that she always wore. Her legs shifted. I took a breath, slipped the pants over her feet. Her butt shook when I moved her. I hoisted her up and she folded into me. I pulled her into bed and tugged a blanket over her chest. I stood there in the light with my hands on my hips. I watched Mom's lips purse and pull.

This fear pulsed. It was old and swinging. It would well up when she woke me in the middle of the night to clean the attic or mow our postage stamp of a half-lawn with the hand mower (we didn't have to mow the whole stamp because it was a duplex. I always just mowed the left, it took about five turns, the right half grew long).

In general, she'd started to go white in the eyes, glassy white.

She had been talking about taking a drive for weeks. She wanted to take a drive. It was May and storming, she wanted a drive. I wanted a drive, too, kind of.

Mom packed the car and we stood on the ridged front walk.

We're going to Jefferson, she said, showing me a collection of portraits she'd printed and framed. The portraits were of thin sepia people, looking stark and dead.

Her plan was to drive us through heavy sheets of humidity, through the piney woods, raking down toward the road. She wanted us to commune with the ghosts of slaves who had been murdered as part of the illegal trade in the region, she wanted us to be together.

We're looking for slave steps, Mom said, holding both of my hands in hers before we got into the car. She was so serious, wet hands.

Mom lined the sepia portraits up on the front seat, asked me to sit in the back. She handed me a map as we pulled onto the highway and put on a tape of spirituals, hymns.

Mom rocked in the front seat. Sunlight drooped. I rubbed my hands on the fabric car seats. A small pioneer town skipped in front of us, dusk curved into the cracked buildings. Mom drove us past the town and onto a weedy dirt road. We bumped along for a mile until she stopped the car and yanked at the emergency break.

Here! she said, pushing at my knee.

Just over the ridge was a slipping series of stone steps growing out from weeds. She pulled out a box from the front seat filled with tea candles and set her portraits on top. She put the box in my arms.

The town smelled like eucalyptus, pine, some rubber, dust. She was silent, her head bowed, Mom asked me to set the box down underneath a tree. She put her finger to her lips as she removed each portrait. She whispered into the glass on each one, kissed all the faces, leaned the portraits against a tree trunk, then swayed toward her box of candles. I watched her move to light them, she was small and shadowed. She handed me a matchbook and wanted me to light a line.

At the site, there were no markers or placards, just ten clear stone steps in a bogged, log-filled wetland slightly out of town that we waded together.

I watched her move silent from candle to candle, trying to exorcise some part of herself, connecting.

If my mother is washing over me like anything not totally intelligible, like a good poem, I read her so differently. I hear her in her own language, not just a version of her run through mine. What if she is more like an event, raking over? This was that. She wanted me to connect me to the pain, to the horror of whiteness. This is the least crazy thing. She has always brushed her hair away from her eyes and taught me about two bodies standing in the wind, solid, unyielding. What's been done will never be undone, her body always said.

* * *

I called Grammy every Saturday, would listen to her chuckle and close my eyes. Her voice was thin. I was afraid to shake it. I didn't tell her that Mom had a new boyfriend and I was put into special ed. I was put into the program in sixth grade, but it wasn't as extreme feeling until high school. When I was a freshmen and we lit things on fire and threw desks out of the windows. Mom smelled so bad, I didn't say that.

When will you be home? I'd ask Mom before she left, while she was holding the phone and moving to write a number down.

Not sure. Call me at Brian's, she'd say, shutting her purse and reaching to kiss me on the side of my face. I'd jerk away, she smelled like trailing alcohol, mint perfume.

She'd wave goodbye. I'd wave back, watching out the window. I'd turn to the kitchen, shaking my head. I'd talk to myself about those assholes and him just getting her fucking drunk, he'd just get her drunk and then who had to take care of her? Fucking me.

A few weeks earlier, Brian brought us to the state fair, bought Mom beer in gigantic plastic cups. We lost her in the stockyards, she was laying down on a haystack near a pen of piglets, squealing at them, clapping for them, getting them to stampede.

I hated this arrangement. His face, he was wet like a pig. I was having trouble concentrating at school. She'd refuse to drive me sometimes, so I'd just stay home, would watch Jerry Springer and heat up frozen tamales.

Once, when Mom was out with Brian, I opened cupboards looking for bottles, any bottle. I pulled a chair to the fridge to reach for a tall glass vodka bottle that I carried down and poured out. I poured the vodka down the drain, talking to myself the whole time, shaking my head.

Before bed that night, I touched myself with a vibrating doodle pen. I'd been hanging out in tornado chatrooms on AOL. I was usually in there, ready to masturbate with anyone or talk about storms. I'd message with Priapis33 and sit on my own hand so that it'd go numb and then I could touch myself as if I was somebody else. I was in bed with the doodle pen, heat zipping through me. I fell asleep like that with pants undone and legs slumped off the mattress.

I woke suddenly when I realized Mom was yelling. I sat up and looked toward the small sailboat-shaped nightlight she'd gotten me.

She was against me before I realized it, grabbing my hair. She clocked me out of bed. I was limp. I banged against the wall. The feeling was jagged, she shook the glass that always seemed to be raking through my belly. I didn't fight her.

What the fuck is wrong with you, she was saying, she was pulling.

She tugged me into the bathroom that was off the hallway and slammed the door. She left me there for a while in the dark. I still hadn't said a word. I didn't answer her because I didn't know. It was so humid that the bathroom floor felt like crying.

A few minutes later, she burst back in and dragged me out, through the living room, past the mirror, past the kitchen, down several concrete stairs into the garage.

In there, Mom turned off the light, closed the door. I lay quiet on the concrete, looked into the dark and fingered a weird adrenaline tranquility. I tried to rub out the sensation of tugged hair. I felt beady, the concrete peeped, humid. I felt naked. I was not, but being dragged out of bed had been so weird that I almost started laughing—

Mom opened the door, slammed on the light. I shielded my eyes.

What did you do with the fucking alcohol? She looked gaunt and ethereal, backlit.

I poured it down the drain, I said into the floor.

She tilted her head.

What?

I watched her mouth, pinched and short.

I poured it out, I shouted.

There was a loud pause. Several cars passed on the street out front, headlights swept across us under the door.

I thought you drank it, she whispered.

I thought you drank it, she said again, nodding.

She stepped down one stair at a time.

Her arms opened.

A tear kicked off my face and into an oil stain.

She gathered me up, pulled me up, put one arm under my knees and my body. She pulled me into her lap. I was spinning. I wanted to rip my fingers off and throw them to her.

When Mom decided I needed to go to church it was around then and she took me to a giant Episcopal church midday on Sunday and told me to stay until she came back. The services were all over. I wandered around until somebody pointed me in the direction of the youth ministry offices. They had a little bowl of "Testamints," a lady named Madeline was at a computer by the door, she shook my hand, gave me a mint and told me to wait for Episcopal Youth Council. Her arm shook like Grammy's. You could come here any-time, but EYC was Sundays at six. Apparently, it was full of kids whose parents were worried about them. I sat there swinging my legs until a girl walked up and shook my hand. She had a lip pierc-ing and a septum piercing and was wearing all black and braids.

I'm gonna show her around, she said to Madeline and grabbed me up out of the chair. I followed her, her flip-flops slapped the linoleum. We turned a corner, she put a finger to her lips, tugged me into a bathroom.

I've got something better than pot, she said and it was a little crumpled silver ball. She unwrapped it and revealed a mound of orange-pink powder, took parts of a pen out of her front pocket and a lighter.

Want to? she asked.

She was nodding while she asked, her face was perfect.

I said sure and she said, Good, we'll do it later. I want to show you around first.

Her name was Ally, she took me to meet a small clump of other kids by the door, a few of them had just been released from juvie for stealing car parts. They were friendly.

You're funny, the girl said, when we were smoking the powder on the far side of the parking lot.

What do you mean?

I fumbled with my mouth near her fingers.

I dunno, you just seem kinda funny, I like it, she said.

I figured that was okay, funny was okay, and drugs were okay because they weren't alcohol and nobody would know anyway.

The powder we smoked was meth, but I didn't feel anything except I wanted to write about her, how she looked like Alicia Keys and how she told me she had sex with her boyfriend at the church sometimes. She was anchored and chiseled, ran away from home for several weeks at a time.

I told her that in special ed, everyone would sell their Adderall to the rich kids in advanced placement. I'd sell my Codeine and buy erasers from the school store that pulled apart like putty. When, we moved to Dallas, they put me on Hydrocodone for the pain and put the script in the nurse's office. Every day at lunch, I'd hold my tray and walk around the cafeteria, looking at the remote hostility in everyone's posture. Sometimes, I'd turn away with my tray, set it back in the rack and walk down to the nurse's office. I'd tell them I was in pain when I was or I wasn't and they'd fit me into a little room with a rubber bed, give me a Dr Pepper, a Tootsie Roll, the Codeine. I'd smile at the ceiling until the end of the school day.

Ally started buying pot from me, and I'd go over to her house to smoke because her parents were never home. She built this smoking room in her closet with leopard-print blankets. We'd go over there on Sundays and pretend to know what we were doing with our hands.

After a few months of this, somebody bought us a six-pack and she and I sat around it, popped all the bottles out of the perforated cardboard and set them between us. She put one bottle near my feet and uncapped it.

Here we go, she said.

I leaned forward, hot and wet   Mom's smell, I winced.

Ally was my first crush aside from the woman from *Bewitched*. I had a serious love for that lady and didn't realize that if I went to the studio where I imagined she was, where I wanted to go, where I imagined that if I just went, I'd be loved by her, she wouldn't be there because she died in 1995.

I was attracted to the danger in this equation. We got to behave badly at church. We were also ignored. And we needed each other.

Ally ran away often, and by the time I was a senior in high school, she'd been in rehab multiple times.

Ally is also the person who taught me how to cut myself. She'd always have long, scabbing cuts on her hands, an odd choice, said the guidance counselor at school when I'd described it to her once.

When I cut myself for the first time, it was after seeing Ally, and I took a pair of needlepoint scissors from the box my mom had for me of sewing things, and I sliced up and down my thumb, right where Ally had hers.

There was a surge of comfort.

Mom was in the other room when this was going on. It seems really simple now, like there is a kind of suspension of reality that I still crave. Who I am thuds against it.

I might be describing adrenaline.

I wonder whenever I touch someone if I'm repeating this hit. I think of it when I touch thigh or cheek, when I'm suddenly intoxicated.

And I think of seagulls, the ones with the red bulb on the end of their beaks, it's a taste bud, they are so sensitive to sugar that when they're exposed to processed food with hugely high sugar content, there's no going back. This is why they are freaks on the beach, taking peanut butter sandwiches out of loose fingers, away from little kids.

Apparently, there's some discussion about how PTSD in childhood creates a permanent drive toward intensity. Maybe this is kind of duh. But I worry that's what's happened. That I am incapable of a kind of calm or that people see all this when they look at me.

"I think about *natural* and *unnatural*, trying to grasp their meanings," writes Clare, "Is an agribusiness cornfield unnatural, a restored prairie natural? How about the abundance of thistle, absence of bison, those old corn furrows? What was once normal here; what can we consider normal now? Or are these the wrong questions?"

I wonder about the mythic place before influence, before trauma or whatever, and how sometimes this idea of a pure kind of "before" gets mixed up with the idea of "natural."

In her book *Against Purity*, Alexis Shotwell cites the copy on a bottle of soap she saw on an airplane—"Purity is natural," said the soap. "We come into this world with all the right instincts. We are innocent, and therefore perceive things as they should be, rather than how they are. Our conscience is clear, our hands clean, and the world at large is truly beautiful."

Yeah, she's saying, but you're using this idea to sell me something.

"The slate has never been clean, and we can't wipe off the surface to start fresh—there's no 'fresh' to start... there is no primordial state we might wish to get back to, no Eden we have desecrated, no pretoxic body we might uncover through enough chia seeds and kombucha," writes Shotwell. "[Purism] is a common approach for anyone who attempts to meet and control a complex situation that is fundamentally outside our control."

Anne Fausto-Sterling does a similar kind of unpacking in her text *Sex/gender: Biology in a Social World* where she builds an argument about preferences in kids for pink or blue.

"How do such preferences develop? The old way of looking at the question is to ask is it nature or is it nurture? Do girls love pink because of something inborn about their visual system?" She goes on to suggest that it's really a dynamic thing and mentions the analogy (first posited by Evelyn Fox Keller) that looks at "the trait 'I love pink' as a 100 gallon bucket of water." She asks, what if nature adds seventy gallons and nurture thirty, then we'd be able to say what percentage is what. But she concludes that's not possible. What if rather than that, nurture is bringing the bucket for nature to fill up, "then what percentage is due to nature and what to nurture? The truth is, the question doesn't make any sense."

Who cares? is another way to get at it.

Sometimes we assume that a binary system of gender needs dis-
mantling the world over, that everyone's equally obsessed with
it. Fausto-Sterling attempts to disassemble this, too, taking apart
the assumption (particularly by white/western feminists) that all
cultures are held to a gender binary as a form of social organiza-
tion. She holds up the work of Nigerian anthropologist Oyeronke
Oyequmi who writes about Yoruba pronouns, for example, which
indicate age rather than gender.

It was kind of a strange thing to do, but I went to Amazon after I read
this and searched "naturalness," just to see. The first item that comes
up in the search is (presumably targeted for me) a book I actually
already have, *There is No Such Thing as a Natural Disaster*; then a
K-cup flavor: Café Vanilla from Café Escapes; Scandinavian Living
Bamboo Toothbrushes, a 4-pack and one free tongue scraper; and
Moovant Silicone Breast form mastectomy prosthesis inserts. I can't
help but think of Haraway. We're all cyborgs at this point.

I once wrote a book about a vacant K-Mart and a woman there
who was feeding hundreds of thousands of birds from the empty
parking lot every day. I wrote it because I'd just moved to LA and
was hating how much it felt like Dallas where everything seemed
plastic. I'd started parking at the lot on my way home every day
to look at the birds. After a few weeks, I showed up to find a series
of permanent signs that lined the lot: "no trespassing or loitering,
feeding birds or wildlife." I started the project because I wondered what "wildlife" meant in this context. I always want to know

what's "natural" about the "unnatural" and all the problematics of that: messiness as perfect too.

Mom was talking to me from the front door, speaking like a child, making squeaking noises like she was excited. She was home from work. I heard her close the door and toss her keys into a bowl. She was saying something about popcorn. Let's make popcorn! she was saying. Mother-daughter night! she called.

I'd smoked pot at lunch. My mouth was chunky and slow. I was waiting for Ally to show up on AOL. Mom'd asked me to vacuum and to unload the dishwasher. I hadn't done either. I listened to her chirp, singing or something. There was a breeze scratching a pecan tree against my window, the duplex jogged against her movement. I heard her walk into the kitchen. It was quiet, she clinked in the kitchen.

Hey, she called, You didn't do anything! You didn't empty the dishwasher or anything. We were supposed to have a night together!

I didn't answer. I was tired of her face and the fact that it was moving toward the floor, getting grayer. She was so thin, she pushed open my door.

I looked at her, she tensed up, I couldn't tell if she was joking.

She had a handful of silverware from the dishwasher at her side,
she smelled wet and pinched, her eyes ran all around.

Then she said something like I'll kill you and the house felt quickly
cool.

She came close, raised her hand, held the silverware up to my face.
I saw my own hand on her stomach. I was pushing. She fell.

I've been thinking a lot about Freud's thing about how happiness
is complete only if "the baby is a little boy who brings the longed-
for penis with him."

I wanted it—the power—does everybody? I wondered about taking
it, taking the control. Holding the universe by the neck and sucking
it out, whispering to it: *when I leave here, it's mine,* you know?

This feeling, the desire to *have it,* is petrifying.

Here, I watch myself confront a certain quality of light I've evaded
thus far in the book: the electric hiss of southern California, cloud-
less sun. Grasses moving through ugly yellow light. Cramped,
windy eucalyptus. Circuses of veins on the backs of legs walking
out of California, south, southwest. I want the hue off of me, dead
moths, hanging drapes.

Various parts seep into focus, I lived in California in 1989. Mom spread a yellow paste on my face. I still have no conception why. I fingered apricots that fell into the yard. I had a bowl cut. She liked to hold me crying, sobbed into my stomach while I stood and she knelt on the wax-orange floor.

Am I sprung from the sour face of this?

Now, I see so much of Mom in the mirror. I took a shower this morning and blood dripped out of me and onto a towel on the floor and it was like someone knocking.

That first night, I fit the hood of my blush-red sweatshirt over my head and lay on a set of bleachers behind a dugout in the park. I put my hands in my pockets and tried to fold my legs under me. I considered taking off my shoes. The sky was perfect, cars cooled, slow. I wondered how to retrieve extra clothes. I looked at the glow of living room on the grass from a home nearby. I looked at my black, burnt Converse sneakers, hanging half off a sliver of riser. I wasn't cold, not warm. I was absent and free. I considered masturbating and my hair moved slightly. I saw something soft happening, close to home and ebullient. I was bright against chunks of grass and gravel. I was night and nighttime. I breathed in adrenaline, some rising.

* * *

The next night, I pulled a brand-new refrigerator box out of the stack that several adults had laid across the lawn of the school. Some of the kids were already decorating theirs, had them leaned near the well-manicured shrubbery at the school's entrance. Someone else set up a hot plate and a pot of soup on the front steps, they had a package of bread and small cups, a bunch of kids were already lined up.

This was a fundraiser for Habitat, the Shack-A-Thon, a week-long event on the front lawn of the school. Students slept in cardboard boxes and raised awareness and money for homeless support. The handful of other students were blonde girls from K-Life, wearing Be-Like-Christ T-shirts, with well-maintained manicures that they nursed all week long, sleeping in their boxes under the supervision of an officer who was staffed by the school to patrol the area.

I pulled my box as far as possible from all the others, made it into a rectangle and crawled inside. We were only supposed to bring our clothes and all that we needed in one paper bag—new paper bags that they handed out at the beginning. I rifled through mine for the ziplock of mushrooms I got from Ally, I was hoping they weren't crushed. I held them up and checked them over.

I slept in my box and dreamt that it was filled with spiders and woke up with the cardboard leaking in, wet clumps on my arms and legs, it was raining. I dragged my stuff under an overhang near the school and found all the blonde girls there, huddled in neon sleeping bags, smiling and sipping soup. They scooted away from me on the step. At the time, I was going through this period where I didn't know what to do with my body. I'd wear something low-cut and odd, my long hair winding down my chest. I'd fling it back, jump into Jeeps with boys. Still, these girls and I were in high contrast.

Once, somebody in the front seat of one of these Jeeps offered me a beer, I was being looked at, I drank it, was warm—I told my friends that it reminded me of communion and they laughed. One of them made a sign of the cross, poured some beer into his hand, splashed it on my face.

That next day, my journalism teacher caught me sleeping at my desk and pulled me into her office. She pointed at her desk when she said, you know, by law, I'm supposed to report things like this. I thought she meant the beer.

.

I was holding a bunch of books at my side. I slid my books onto her desk and sat down in the chair opposite hers. I put my elbow on her desk and my chin in my hand.

Ok, I said, what do you want me to do?

I was writing in my notebook in the first row of English class when a man with a walkie-talkie jutted his head through the classroom door. He looked up at my teacher, a blonde, small woman wearing a blue paisley dress. She pointed to me.

I looked up at her.

She seemed to pull herself back, moved papers around on her desk.

The man with a walkie-talkie waited for a second, then seeing my hesitation, moved into the room and hooked me by the arm. He led me out, one hand on my elbow, the other holding the walkie-talkie near his mouth.

The man opened the door to a room I'd never noticed near the entrance of the school. The blinds were drawn and the man pulled out a chair for me at a wooden desk across from a gray woman in red clothes, sitting over a large tape recorder. So, we are Child Protective Services, she said. Do you know why we are here?

They looked blankly at me, we all looked blank.

My stomach was hard. The light in the room was out of control, slipping under the shades, hitting a crystal paperweight on the desk, a gray blotter, hitting me.

This was an accident—the man and the woman from CPS, their pursed lips, their grubby nails, that ugly room, the clicking of their tape recorder slow, sweet.

* * *

I have a good friend who this happened to, too, we met at Naropa when we were both scholarship recipients for their Summer Writing Program, they were the Zora Neal Hurston award recipient and I was the Kari Edwards one. When we realized we shared CPS in our background, my friend told me they'd been taken right away and shoved into a group home and then moved through foster care. This didn't happen to me.

My mom was a nice white lady who went to church. Nobody listened to my friend's mom. My friend eventually moved in with a foster family in New York that they're close to. We share a lot of things, but not this. Whiteness made it so they interviewed my mom and then told me not to go home, that was it.

I didn't believe it, really, and so, I went home to get some things, or to try to when I thought Mom was at work. She wasn't, she was home, and when I opened the gate to go in, she caught me between the gate and the door and said I was scum, I'd never be her daughter. I'd ruined it. I stood there with my backpack slung off my shoulder and felt burnt-out. Her eyes were big and blue, it looked like she'd been crying. You called them on me, she kept hissing, we're done. She stabbed her fingernail in the air.

It's impossible to be a mother. I was a flame in the corner lighting up all of Mom's mistakes. I'd say, Mom, I know what you're doing and she'd slam her bedroom door at me. No one means to be like this, me either, I didn't know how to be a kid. I just decided to be homeless for a while, I'd stay at the church sometimes or with a youth minister, I slept on one of their porches, stayed in the park. I didn't know how long this would last.

A girl from newspaper staff asked me if I wanted to have a sleepover and I was into the idea. She was decent and I was lonely. I said yes even though she always kept her hair high on her head. She was always shaking her head. I got into her Volvo. I leaned my seat far back, crossed my arms over my chest.

She pulled onto the freeway.

I glanced at her. Her knuckles, her jaw, seemed tight. I looked out the window and watched as we got on a ramp aimed out of town.

Your house is this way?

She shook her head.

A few days earlier, she'd caught me jabbing at myself in the empty journalism office with the leather punch part of a pocketknife. A few weeks before, she watched while I sat on the bleachers during an away game, I'd joined the softball team as a way to fulfill my school's

P.E. credit. I'd known the coaches since middle school, since the other kids would call them dykes and hide from them in the locker room. Still, in middle school I'd go sit at the park, on the bleachers, put my chin in my hand, watch their high school practices and imagine being on the team. I wasn't athletic at all, so when I did join the team, they let me sit on an upside-down Home Depot bucket and keep the book. They were nice to me, it gave me somewhere to go after school and get the credit I needed without having to run or do anything else. I was still miserable though, and the same girl who saw me before with the leather punch saw me take apart one of my reporter's notebooks, leave a long thread of wire, and whack at my arm with it. She and a couple of my other teammates walked up, I didn't stop. I didn't care.

You cut yourself all the time in front of people, she said. It's weird. I'm taking you to Baylor.

What?

She glanced at me as she pulled up to the outpatient entrance of the squat city hospital.

You've lost your mind, I said.

I'm calling my mom, she said.

I started to laugh, a big full laugh. A handful of stars were gathered on the horizon, streetlamps loomed over the nearly empty lot. She yanked her car into park. I crossed my legs. She looked at me and nodded. I'm putting my mom on speaker phone.

She took off her seatbelt and sat up straight in the front seat of the Volvo. Her mom didn't answer. I kept my eyes closed.

I told them I wasn't suicidal while she sat in the waiting room. The doctors looked at the small scratches on my arms and sighed, rolled their eyes even. It's benign, they told the girl as they walked me out. She seemed almost angry.

Was this some Christian thing? I asked her while we walked back to her car. She said no, was just trying to help. She wouldn't drop me off at the park with the bleachers where I wanted to go and she wouldn't bring me to her house. So, I offered her Hank's. My stepdad's, I said, even though he wasn't anymore.

When we pulled up the block, I could see a chessboard in the window, turned toward the street, a cracked window, reeking plants moved up the wall, a feathered pecan tree blew. Mom hadn't wanted me to go over there, not since she and I moved to the duplex, even though it was on the same highway just a mile down.

I knocked, shifted my weight on the cracked concrete step. Hank came to the door smiling. The girl stayed in her car and he waved at her. I stepped inside to talk to him. She idled. I told him my friend was nuts and was trying to admit me to a hospital for cutting myself. Hank was chewing on something, looked like he was waiting or thinking, I couldn't tell. He took my arm in his hand and pulled up my sleeve, moved his thumb across a small swatch of scars, spidering up and away. We stood there like that for a long time, with my friend, well-lit, looking at us in the rearview mirror.

In the counseling office at my high school, I was put into the cutter group. There were ten of us who were called out of class once a week to sit in a windowless room and discuss our feelings. After two weeks, one of my fellow members handed me a quarter-folded piece of paper. The person said they were transgender. They'd written a poem for me. I thought it meant they had all the genitals and I wondered why they'd written to me. That day, I threw out anything I owned with any kind of rainbow on it.

I was slowly walking and smoking near the outside of school when a car pulled up next to me. It was Hank. He rolled down the window and asked me to get in, I did.

We're having a meeting, he said, shifting gears quietly.

When we pulled up at the church, the gray woman from CPS waved us over to a bench near the entrance. She was standing next to a man dressed as a priest, Mom, her hair lifted in the breeze, and Mom's boyfriend.

Hank turned off the car and lifted the parking brake. There were birds moving overhead, a sweet, dirty smell, fast food frying.

Want to come live with me? He swung his driver side door open and one leg out.

During our talk, Mom's boyfriend suggested that I live wherever I could best do my homework. Mom was silent. I watched the corners of her mouth move slightly. She looked thinner, harder, held her hands in her lap. Hank suggested that I go live with him. The priest and social worker nodded. I looked at Mom, her eyes were off and away, not looking at me. One of her hands had moved up to hold her wrist.

When it was all over, I got in Hank's car and Mom got in hers with her boyfriend. I watched an emptiness wash around. From inside Hank's car, I saw Mom's shoulders curl. She seemed to be sobbing, her body jerked in the passenger seat. She brought her hands to her face, brushed her hair back from her eyes.

Bile rose in my throat.

Does she have to live here? Tye said. He said it with half of his mouth on a straw, cherry limeade. He put all his weight on one hip and crossed his arms like *you*.

By the time I moved in with them, the boys had gotten huge, Tye was shaped like a linebacker, Gunner, too, they had shaggy hair and hormones and handfuls of friends that they'd play video games with. They would turn away from me whenever I walked into a room. They would complain loudly to Hank. I used to cry into our separation, the violence of genetics. Sometimes Hank would break up our fighting, otherwise he'd sigh and go work on my room.

He was building me a room by hand where there'd been a porch, it was sheetrock and plywood with an immaculate, blue-tinted glass sliding door. He bought me an airbed and a blanket. Even after he was finished, he'd still walk by and sand something occasionally.

My brothers are both happy for the most part these days. We spend some holidays together. I wish we were closer sometimes, but our relationship seems to deepen as we age and as I relax into my fears around their acceptance of me. They don't ask me about anything, gender just falls like a blanket across the couch. We all sit around and watch sports. No one says anything.

Except, not long ago, Tye called to say he has a colleague who is into experimental poetry. Apparently he told the colleague that he knows someone who does that professionally. You, he said. And would it be okay if he gave his colleague my email? I was so warmed by his acknowledgement that I have a place in his mind. It was something like respect.

The truth is, my grandmother's question about Mom liking them more drums around, our childhood did shape me, like one of a number of nodes. I have tried to win their approval, to win them into my life. I don't think my gender is this trying, but I have no idea.

When I lived with them and on nights when Hank was home early from work, we'd go on rides through the neighborhood. The boys would stay home and play video games. He'd drive me through the alley behind Mom's house. Just to see, he said.

She'd always be in there, the lights on, we'd see through the fence that she was wearing lace, pouring wine, the house raw and empty.

At this point, I'd told a group of friends that I didn't want to count drinks my whole life, I heard that's what alcoholics had to do. I was looking up into the sky from some field out of town when I said it. They nodded at me without looking up because they weren't listening, doing bong rips instead with their shirts off surrounded by yellow grass. I stood up, brushed my hands on my pants, said something about going to get a fake ID, and walked off.

This guy I was dating had driven me to a place on Jupiter Road. I'd said we were dating and that I'd dated other people before, but I didn't do anything with him besides drugs. Everyone said I was a dyke but didn't know it and I'd drink at them whenever they talked like that.

The place on Jupiter Road sold two fake IDs for $125. The boy waited in the car for me. The little shop was inset into a strip mall with blacked-out windows, there was a little DMV vignette set up inside, a blue background and a camera. They asked me for my money through a plastic slot and I gave it to them, asked me to choose my state and whether or not I was an organ donor. I said New Orleans, Louisiana, and yes, and stood in front of the blue background.

When they printed the ID, I rubbed my thumb across the photo. I looked old, my hair was a little gray in the light. I had a black T-shirt on, my favorite one, and my hair was wavy, almost pretty. My thin mouth was smiling slightly. I covered my eyes with my thumb, without the green eyes and this hair, I looked just like Mom.

I had a dream not long ago about a long-corded phone covered in crepe streamers.

In the dream, I eat my own hand like an ouroboros.

I used to have the same dream as a kid except it was a snake like the Nokia cellphone game going across a white screen, that was it, and prior to the game coming out. The dream figure was the line of pixels that sped up, along with a murmur of voices in the back. They would speed to yelling, a deep voice and a soft voice talking over each other, screaming eventually.

Whenever I'd tell an adult I'd had a bad dream, the only way I knew to explain it was that the line had gone too fast.

I wish someone would have asked me to draw it.

It's odd when time works like a modular couch, thin and carpeted. I've played these scenes over and over in my mind and I can't make them full, can't shake them out, they're flat in my memory.

Here's the insanity: I saw this happening and couldn't stop myself from going exactly that way.

I'll never forget walking into this liquor store when I was eighteen or something, there was the weird milk smell like always. I marched around with a thirty rack of beer in one hand, a plastic jug of vodka in the other. The Mike's Hard sign flashed yellow onto my car, my friends waiting in it.

The guy at the counter looked at me, looked at my ID. He looked too long. Heat rose in my hands. He pushed the ID back to me across the counter—this is fake, he said.

It isn't—I started.

It is, he said.

I went to grab it and he pulled it back. His knuckles were white.

We'd better keep this, he said, pointing up at the camera. He scratched his skullcap with his thumb.

Don't come back here until you're legal, dear.

I wanted to cry but I smirked instead, laughed as I walked to my car. I leaned in and told everybody I could still get alcohol, I'd get somebody to buy for us. Hold on.

I drove us to a house where this woman always answered her door in a towel. Her place was a small building, had a plywood door. I knocked. A dog barked. It was so cold. I knocked again. Her car wasn't there. The street was silent except for me. The woman had several wet pots on her front step, a wet welcome mat.

I hit the door with my fist. I pushed against the window by the door, just to try it, I put my body against it. No movement. I banged again. A plastic horse missing its front two legs was laying on the step next to the pots, a deflated football.

I looked at my friends in the car, they were messing with the radio.

I slid down the wall and sat. The wet welcome mat bled into my jeans. I leaned my head against her door. It was freezing. The welcome mat smelled sick.

I couldn't stop when I started and that's about the whole of it.

Drugs were fine but alcohol made something gorgeous happen to me, bright grass, a purple night, the warmest coup. I knew I shouldn't, because of Mom and everything, but there was no room for what I should be doing. I was in crisis. Nothing was happening but everything felt like crisis.

Sometimes when my dog is startled these days, she bolts, I've seen her do it a handful of times, once was when the fire alarm in the house went off, another was when someone strange walked up the back stairs. She just starts running, if she's outside and I'm not careful, she'll tear down the street and into the road. She's blind running. When I caught her the last time, she was two blocks away, cars were stopped on all sides while she zig-zagged into the road and out. When I picked her up, she looked resolutely grateful because she was startled even by her own escape, dazed.

Freud writes about the love impulse as tangled up with destruction, bent toward annihilation, which is either expressed outwardly, as in sadism, or inward.

He wasn't as homo-hating as I always thought. Some see him as the father of clinical "treatment" of homosexuality, but Freud himself didn't view queerness as a disease. He famously advised the anxious mother of a gay son that homosexuality "is nothing to be ashamed of, no vice, no degradation; it cannot be classified as an illness; we consider it to be a variation of the sexual function."

Still, Freud did believe that homosexuality resulted from a disruption of the "normal" pattern of child development, shaped in early childhood. For Freud, no one was naturally homosexual or heterosexual.

So many people, clinicians and laypeople, have taken this as fact. Gay was only removed from the DSM in 1973.

I was hanging out with my friend today and I told them about the premise of this book—we've been friends for a decade or so now and they said they've never equated their sexuality or their gender with any of their trauma or thought of it as causal.

Later they were reflecting on a project they wanted to make, voice recordings of healing sessions with their spiritual advisor combined with images alluding to abuse they suffered. I am worried people will connect those two things and make it seem like I'm trans because of that, they said, then, Oh, that's what you mean…

I found myself like this:

I was wearing a dirty corduroy coat and a blue trucker cap with a nappy slot for a Polaroid, there was a photo of a naked boy in there, an old boyfriend of mine flexing in the bathtub, wet and blue.

In the waiting room of the free clinic, I'd written on the form that I was having "homoerotic fantasies that I want to curtail" and leaned back in the orange-carpeted waiting room chair, put the ballpoint pen back onto the plastic clipboard. My boots dripped on the carpet. I smelled like my wet hat, wet rabbit and beer. The gurgling fish tank lit weird water onto the wall.

I needed counseling. I wanted someone so badly to be on the other side of me, looking. The subtle discomfort I'd always known had grown cacophonous, drumming around in my head almost constantly. I couldn't do school. I couldn't do life, apparently. I'd moved out after high school, had been to three different colleges on the East Coast. I'd dropped out, flunked out, was asked to leave. After dropping out of the first one a month in, I ended up sleeping at an uncle's on the bottom of my cousin's bunk bed outside of New York City and working at Starbucks. I went to a commuter school after that for a minute and failed out with a .99 GPA. I'd dated a boy. We were in and out of trouble. I broke up with him to come up to this rural state school and start over. I'd left high school with a scholarship from special ed and lost the whole thing, I got another, was about to lose it too.

In the waiting room, with the clipboard on my lap, I ran my index finger along a cut on the back of my hand. It was from waking up in a tree. I'd come out of a blackout wearing a Joan of Arc costume that I didn't remember buying or putting on. The tree was dripping, I ached, my head ached, I shook my head, put my hand on my forehead—Mom's hands were always bleeding, dry hands for some reason, cracked and bleeding. I pictured her waving. I didn't know where she was and I didn't want to talk about it.

We hadn't spoken since I moved away, two years or so. Mom was dating somebody new, maybe had married again, I wasn't sure.

I'd gone to the counseling office on campus because the one person I'd made friends with thought I was trying to have sex with her, didn't want to hang out anymore.

For months she watched while I played cards with a group of boys in a room at the edge of the woods and would eye me. I'd smooth my arms out on the green fuzz table and smell my hands: cigarettes, orange juice. The boys would slap their hands on their pants and say, she fucking beat us again. Get her more fucking drunk next time. I'd put some dip in my cheek and the girl would smile, we'd pass out together in bed, her warm ass in my stomach, our drunken stomachs—

Then nothing. No calls. Two or three days went by. I saw her walk out to the parking lot with a handful of blonde girls, they were laughing, throwing their heads back, she put her hand on one girl's sleeve, I saw her, she saw me and her face twisted, the girls tugged her into the car. They peeled away toward a line of wet trees, the parking lot fanned out.

All of myself careened around. My insides were mutable, watery. A guy was walking up the steps of the building wearing full camouflage and carrying two dead ducks by the neck. A swatch of black birds blew from the roof to a tree. I crunched through the thin trail of snow to my room, pulled open the door and stomped up the wet stairs to my white, peeling fridge. I grabbed a few beers, put them into my coat pockets. I got a joint from my desk drawer and stuck it behind my ear, pulled myself through my window and onto the metal roof overhang. It smelled like rain. I dangled my feet. People were walking around under my feet, walking to eat. All the lights were coming on. My room was dark. My eyes were red.

When I went to her room, it was hours later, and I was holding a bottle around the neck, a glass Orloff bottle from under my bed. She didn't answer when I knocked. The carpet zoomed, I staggered around, listening to laughter. I slammed the bottle against her door—I think it was her door. It evaporated. I slid down the wall, still holding the neck, a shard.

I'd just seen the movie about Johnny Cash with Joaquin Phoenix. Johnny Cash, in the thick of his addiction, woke up in the bed in June Carter's house, he was sweating and writhing and she nursed him, brought things to his bedside. It was so sweet, his sweaty sheets. This is love, it seemed to say.

I took the shard and held it to my forearm, too white. I closed my eyes, leaned my head against the wall, raked the broken glass along my arm, it opened into a mouth like a flower.

The idea of dependence, an addiction to adrenaline, scares the shit out of me. That I could be tugged against my will toward predisposition. I looked at myself in the bathroom mirror at the counseling center before going into the group therapy they'd assigned me to, and I felt this kind of awful nexus of my sexuality and my childhood come together. I'd been so dependent on Mom partially because we'd moved so much, but also partially because we're so similar and actually make a great team.

When we were in New London, she'd wanted to go to Sturbridge Village. It was a couple of hours from us and had a reenactment farm with old equipment and apple bobbing and everything like that. On the way there, she'd put on a tape of train sounds so we could pretend to be going there an old-fashioned way. I held my notebook and was glad for the trees. We got there and they yoked us—it was a thing you could do, pretend to plow. Everything smelled so good and they put this wood harness on the two of us like oxen and we tugged at this metal plow dug into the field. We bumped each other and tugged, laughing, we pretended to pass out to end it.

I've been watching the film *Violette* about Violette Leduc and

Simone de Beauvoir and their relationship. Leduc is the author of *La Bâtarde*, which I've held as a sort of map for years, it's her 1964 bestselling memoir that details Leduc's relationship with her mom and a budding queerness. Her exposure of her mother is undeniable beauty:

"I wind my hair around my curlers, my fingers are telling me what you were like at twenty-five, telling me about your blue eyes, your black hair, your sculptured bangs, your shawl, the tulle, your big hat, my suffering when I was five. My elegant one, my uncrushable one, my courageous one, my vanquished one, my rambling one, my eraser to rub myself out with, my jealous one, my justice, my injustice, my commander, my shy one. What are people going to say? What are people going to think? What would they say? Our litanies, our transfusions."

The tension I suck on throughout is the sensuousness of the language used for her mother, their joined-ness, their union juxta-posed with a queer narrative, her brushing hands with a boarding school friend and then the chunk of pages Leduc spends on the lurid love affair that follows, sneaking into her friend's bed.

I am struck by this juxtaposition and the price of it in my own life, bravery is a word I hate used on my behalf, but for Leduc, it does feel like *La Bâtarde* is a kind of "fuck you" to anxiety—like, I'm just writing this fucking thing, yes, I'm exposing my mother-daughter relationship and its complicated closeness in tandem with my love for women. I don't care if they are equated or faulted or whatever. The sensuousness of the language hangs in the air, no explanation, only a romantic overlay that seems divorced from an anxiety around claims of causality.

Leduc's writing seems to suggest that maternal intimacy and identity formation can happen at once.

Truly, I hate how regularly causality of some kind is floated. Like, once, I was elbowed by a family friend who said, You've probably got hot mom syndrome. He pointed to the oversized suit I was wearing when he said it. This was a family friend who knew my mom as a teenager and he was elbowing me at my paternal grandpa's funeral. Man, I would've liked to get with her, he said.

My grandmother, when she wonders about this, is turning the same camera on my mom that she turned on herself. I know she lives with the anxiety that she did something to cause my mother's pain, made her someone who'd hurt herself. We pass this anxiety around.

In the film *Violette* the actor plays Leduc as cranky and needy, she stomps and throws books around and gets crazed. At one point, trying to connect with de Beauvoir, her unrequited crush at this moment in the film, she yells at de Beauvoir's landlord to let her in to see if de Beauvoir is lying about being on a trip, her suspicion. When she finds a cleaning woman inside the apartment instead of de Beauvoir, she ends up screaming at her, too, and trying to force herself inside. It's like she has a fever.

The next scene is her in bed with her mother, having let her mother live with her and share a bed. After bottoming out with another man, presumably, Leduc awakens from kissing de Beauvoir in a dream, sits upright, looks at her mother, and then moves off the bed to the floor. Here, the film portrays Leduc as internalizing a kind of pathology, an anxiety around correlation or "cause." I turned the movie off.

When Nelson writes of matricide in *The Art of Cruelty*, she raises Kristeva's "violent expulsion of the maternal."

"And while the abjection of the maternal may be necessary, according to Kristeva, to form a subject, its expulsion can never be seamlessly accomplished," Nelson writes. In Kristeva's thinking, Nelson explains, "the abjected maternal returns, via horror, repulsion, the uncanny, haunting, melancholia, depression, guilt, the inchoate but harrowing sense that one has lost, left or killed something critical."

Nelson goes on to critique this lens. Sure, she concedes, maybe modernity is defined as celebrating dissociation from the mother as a route to individuation as Kristeva suggests. But, Nelson argues, "as with most psychoanalytical concepts, the question of whether they are descriptive, prescriptive, transiently useful, or simply lunatic always strikes me as wide open."

I'd grown up thinking of Mom so much, she was the thing on my mind most. I had to get her out, so I'd put some drugs and drinking there, and then started putting other people in that place. Nothing was working through.

As part of a treatment I undergo for this genetic condition that Mom, Grammy, and I have, I work with this meditation teacher. She has me lie down for twenty minutes a day and welcome the pain. The aim is to let the pain be there, allow it in, invite it in, sit next to it.

The teacher is soft-spoken and slight, she lives with the complications of Polio and is always cold. She is also queer. When I met her for the first time, she talked about realizing she was queer like an enormous feeling in her chest, yellow, and not knowing what to do. I was intrigued by her portrayal of revelation happening inside her body—my understanding of the world had always stopped at the horizon of mine.

She's convinced me over the years that there's an extra amount of hurt in my joints that results from me trying to get rid of the sensations, chase them out, fix them. With her, I sit at my body's bedside.

Now, Grammy struggles to walk and spends most of her time in a wheelchair and Mom goes to bed just as it's getting dark (sometimes that's as early as 4 p.m. in the winter) to maximize morning, her joints hurt less in the morning, mine too.

All three of us have had to learn the complexity of this influence. All of us remind each other of the throbbing, we've all done it. When Grammy held a pack of frozen peas to my head when I was eight and said, Oh, looks like you've got what we have, she sealed it.

Grammy doesn't like to talk about it. She doesn't like to talk about Mom either. I can't remember the last time the three of us were together even though they live only a handful of hours away from each other. My grandparents decided to move further south toward better hospitals and better weather.

I'm so proud of you, Grammy said the last time I was there. You know that, right? We're so proud. You're really a good person.

Except, when I was drinking, Grammy would feed me pot roast with cut carrots and put *Rebecca* on. I wouldn't be able to keep my eyes open. I'd fall asleep before the movie ended. Grammy would have to shake me awake, put her arm around me to help me up the stairs.

Maybe let up on those cigarettes, she'd say, they're making a mess in your car.

She was looking at all the burn holes, yellow foam lining pierced burnt rounds in the fabric. The holes lined the driver's seat, the backseat, too, from when friends would pull me out from behind the wheel and shove me in the back to keep me from driving.

I love you, I'd say.

I love you, too—too much, she'd say.

Only once did she say something and it wasn't about drinking, it was when she was afraid I was still cutting myself, she grabbed my arm in the front yard and pulled my sleeve up.

You're not still doing that to yourself are you?

I hadn't been.

She rubbed at her eyes and said she was sorry.

I don't want to worry, she said, but I do.

Her care for me was crushing. When I tried to shove Mom out of my psyche, I realized it stripped me of this caring, too, of my capacity to feel it and give it back.

Like the meditation teacher thing, I can't get rid of this. I have to connect, rather than dissociating or tossing anybody out. I have to become friendly.

They talk about alcoholism sometimes as a selfish disease. I saw a guy recently who was wasted, he almost backed his car into mine, a tiny house, actually, is what he was driving. I was parked on a hill in the Bay Area and just watched this purple tiny house with a peaked roof back toward me. I had almost a foot behind me, between mine and another car, but I didn't back up, I sat in the driver's seat with my arms folded. The people with the tiny house got within an inch of my bumper and then came around to apologize, it was a couple in their late fifties maybe, and the guy was drunk but in a friendly way. He started crying at one point and the helplessness on his face was familiar. It was the face of a person dying, gesturing like a toddler, clinging to his partner, eyes rolling. If alcoholism is selfish, it's a specific kind, like drowning.

I still think all the time of Grandmother's question, *Did she do this to you*, accompanied by the undeniable background ask, *What are you going to do about it?*

I'd much rather know that there's nothing that was or wasn't done.

This book isn't about individuation or even coming of age, the achievement of selfhood despite everything, it's about ways to find a response, to respond to her.

III.

was always butch, baby butch, stone. Like, don't touch me!
Don't touch me, except touch is all I want. Look, this is
what I always want. Look, this want is who I am.

The only time I ever took testosterone, it was 2008 and I finished reading the *Cyborg Manifesto* and I decided that I was really
rakish. I'd met these kids who were trans and they started calling me
Christopher and *he* and I was the happiest around them I'd ever been.

I decided on surgery. It was right away and after a boy named
Elliot wandered up to me, he was walking away from the sun,
had a buzz cut, a thin sweater.

When he introduced himself, he said, Nice harmonica.

I had a little one hanging around my neck.

He'd just had surgery, he told me, and all he felt like doing was flying.

Nice sweater, I said, because I meant nice chest.

We sat in a tent pitched on the lawn of this low-residency college we were both trying out and he played my harmonica.

That night, we sang a song about wanting to be houseboys, harmonized and everything, made a video of it that he showed everyone on his laptop.

These people pulled me out of bed in the middle of the night to sing it and look at the moon.

There you go, Christopher, they sang.

Within a 24-hour period of getting home, I went to a Poz friend of mine from work who'd been offering me his little tubes of prescription cream.

He left one of his tubes in my box in the mailroom and the next morning, I took a shower and slathered it like moisturizer, put some on my butt because I always thought my butt was seen as too feminine.

I smelled so strongly of the cream at work, a pinkish chemical smell. I went to the bathroom to try and wash it off, let my pants down and wiped my butt with a paper towel. I threw up in that same bathroom a few hours later. I had put too much on. Everything lurched up my throat. I stumbled out of work and took the train home, went back to my apartment and texted a woman who I was trying to get to love me: I'm poisoned, I said.

She picked me up in a cab and held my head in her lap as we rode back to Manhattan. She hauled me up the four-floor walkup and I projectile vomited in her apartment for hours.

We read the tube of testosterone and realized that I was only supposed to squirt a dime-sized amount onto one of my thighs. I worried it counted as a relapse, she rubbed my back.

New York was an expanse of potential. At least, it seemed that way. I'd moved there for it. My first job there was at a holistic center on Crosby and Broome. My boss was a butch trapeze artist with a tan bicep bigger than my face, her name was Lollo, she smiled whenever they called her *he* on our trips to Home

Depot (she called it Homodepot) and I was petrified of her. I once found that she'd been waiting at the door while I was trying to unclog a toilet, shit boiling up to the lid. That same day, she saw me break half a dozen lightbulbs, trying to change them with this ten-foot claw thing that I couldn't keep upright. She patted me on the head, gave me my first copy of *The Well of Loneliness*. I figured she hated me, and I mostly hid from her all day, hid behind doors, in cupboards, in the cubbies where we kept the massage tables.

I was thinking of my fear of Lollo and pulling at my shirt, I felt greasy, I wanted to look cute, when I walked out of my apartment and stepped between two parked cars. I looked both ways, but not really, took four steps toward the street and heard someone yell.

I looked around.

A commercial van was breaking down the block and I didn't have time to move, I made myself into a ball. That's all I remember, some guy saying, Oh shit, and me thinking, Oh shit what?

I woke on the concrete face up, I didn't know how I ended up on my back with bloody knees. Morning sunlight was making its way through the buildings. The pavement was cold. Red and blue lights were flashing on my face. A crowd of people looked down. I was awake.

Come get onto this, somebody said, gesturing at me with a stretcher. Can you get up?

Of course I can get up, I said, and fell.

I was bleeding a little from my cheek and a lot from my knees, people peeled me up from the concrete and my body revealed a puddle of shit, mine, all of the neighbors came out to see.

When we made it to the hospital, I was given a bed and a gown. I threw my underwear away in the stall next door and looked into the mirror. My eyes were red and I had a cut on my cheek. I wondered if this was aloneness, this bridge between myself and circumstance. Who should I call? I lay there for so long, stared at the ceiling, the yellow sink. I needed a cigarette. The curtain between myself and somebody else swished, everything was yellow. I was wet. I took off my gown, little pastel leaves on it, and folded it up on the bed. I needed to get to work. This was taking so long. I pulled on my jeans, found my wallet and my keys in a bowl by the sink, put them into my pocket and ducked into the hall.

I ripped at the hospital bracelet as I walked to the stairwell, squinting because I had a headache, I was limping too. I put my headphones on and rolled a cigarette. I didn't need the hospital, I figured, I was fine. I posted up in front of the bus stop. I didn't know where I was exactly. I leaned against the chain link fence surrounding the hospital and it gave. I guessed at how to get home, put the cigarette in my mouth and clicked through my phone. My cheek was bleeding. I didn't know who to tell. An ambulance railed past, someone next to me spit onto the curb.

I'm alive, I gchatted a different crush, which seemed benign. She was at work and so sent a black cab for me. I got in it a half hour later. I didn't need anybody, I told myself, just somebody's attention. The cab took me back to her mixed concrete and steel loft in Williamsburg and left me there. I was out of place.

When she got home, we went up to the roof to smoke, I held the bottle of 400 mg ibuprofen that she'd picked up for me. She crossed her legs and leaned back, said something about being surprised that I wasn't as manly as she'd thought.

I was too tired to get defensive. I stared at the end of my cigarette.

You're pretty much a muffin, she said, flicking ashes off the roof. You're needy, too, which is also a little surprising, or maybe it's not.

Her mouth and her eyes were at the skyline, she was talking about me to the city.

You should quit your job, you hate your life, she said.

You should be writing, she flicked her cigarette into the Bustelo butt can next to the water tower, folded her arms, stood up.

What are you talking about? I laughed into my closed fist. I loved this.

You really should, she said, turning away from the wind toward the metal stairs. I pulled my coat around my neck.

I called Mom. She answered her cell phone from that camper parked on the periphery of the graveyard. Over the phone, I heard the slap of screen door. It was the place where she'd moved after her episode in Texas with the dip tins and the cherry-faced woman. She answered and I said hi Mom and something lurched in my throat.

It had been two years since I'd gone to visit her in rehab on the East Coast, where she had been shipped to from Texas. I'd heard she weighed eighty-nine pounds or something and I didn't want to look at her—a leaf in a little kid's hand.

It's hard to explain my shakiness—

That idea I was full of, the *don't touch me* one, moved in tandem with my desire to scrape all big emotion off the table.

Mom's love for me has always been the most painful part of my body, a stigmata kind of.

When I called her, she said she'd come right down and I was like, are you kidding? It was a seven-hour drive or something. She said I'd visited her when she needed somebody and maybe she should return it.

Not long ago, I had a call with her about my plans to come visit. We were far along in the planning, I'd gotten the flight and rented a car, but by the end of the conversation, she was saying, Our phone calls are just as good. I don't need to see you and I was sort of like, well fuck and I hung up feeling sorry for myself. I was walking around with the dog and she'd stopped to shit and so I stopped too. I put my phone back in my pocket and looked up. The clouds were so good that day, they never are in LA, but that day they were big and swirling and I remembered New London and all the talking I did to Grammy about the weather. I remembered something Mom had said at the beginning of the conversation about how she didn't really want me to fly or drive because it had been an extra bad winter and was snowy and icy. This is the part I hadn't heard, my brain skipped over it while she was talking. It leaked back in afterward. She'd said: I'd rather you be safe than I see you. I was so busy anticipating her dislike of me that I'd missed it, she was saying she wanted me to be safe, that she was worried about me, I love you, is what it was.

In 2006, when I visited her in rehab, there was a caramel-colored Mercedes in the parking lot outside of the building and a mani-cured hedge that ringed the entire outside. It was bougie. I'd been watching my stomach move on the way there, and when I pulled up to the place, the pressure was too much. I threw up by the car, onto the Mercedes's front tire, and then again in the hedge. I walked, totally nauseous, to the front door of the place, a white-yellow building with another hedge.

I rang the buzzer, shifted the weight from foot to foot.

I said into the intercom, I'm here to visit Marie, and my voice jogged all around. I wanted to cry kind of. My heart was beating in my stomach. I didn't know if we still hated each other.

A woman in beige pants and a purple shirt opened the door and smiled at me. Her name tag swung across her breasts, Welcome in! she said. You here to see your mom?

Yep, I just found out she was here.

Well, I'm sure she'll be glad to see you, she said, walking ahead of me through a hallway.

She pushed another door with her elbow. It opened onto an ivy-coated brick patio sprinkled with iron tables. I looked across the patio. I shielded my eyes.

She should be around here somewhere, the woman said, looking with me.

All the blood in my body went into my stomach.

At the table farthest away beneath a yellow umbrella was a woman reading, her head was bent, she was bottle-blonde and small, she sucked on her knuckle for a second, then pulled her lips into a small child's smile.

I took a long, slow breath, hating my want. My hair moved in the wind and I watched Mom smiling until the woman said, There she is, sweetheart, go say hi.

Mom looked up. She looked trapped and excited, a mutual pressure. Her eyes were clear and worn. She brought her hands to her stomach.

Hey Mom, I said, I came to visit you.

Her mouth was open, more like cooing than like shock or surprise.

I'll let you two say hi, the woman said, and turned back toward the door. I watched the lady leaving and didn't want her to go. I didn't know what to say.

Are you—how are you? Mom started, then stopped. She reached for my hand and held it. I'm so glad to see you, she said, and I let her hold my hand, hard and important. She rubbed her thumb across my fingers.

Want to sit here with me for a minute? She patted the table.

Course, I said.

This is my favorite table, she said, can you see the bird feeder?

I nodded. She pointed through the branches to a thin maple tree that held a small yellow feeder. The feeder was painted to match her rehab.

That's great, Mom, I said.

The same woman from earlier picked up a tray that had been emptied of cookies from a table by the door, several people were scattered around the patio, a few got up to get the ends of coffee, left books piled on tables behind them. It was suddenly summer.

Coffee time is almost over everybody, the woman said from the doorway, she held open a clean screen door.

What's after coffee time?

Nap, Mom said.

That makes no sense.

She laughed and leaned in. Do you think, the next time you come, she said softly, you could bring me some Diet Coke?

She squeezed my hand again.

Just one can or something, she said, we're not allowed to have it.

She leaned back, smiling. I said yes, of course, and she rubbed her thumb across my fingers, hard and happy, I had a cut on one of my fingers, she rubbed it, a small amount of blood creamed through.

For a while, I believed in DNA testing. I thought maybe I carried behavior like this, gender in me like epigenetics, like alcoholism, my mitochondria. But I read *Fantasies of Identification: Disability, Gender, Race* by Ellen Samuels, and Kim Tallbear's work, *Native American DNA*, which details the "semiotics" of blood, its symbol and the legacy—the conflation of blood with genetics. Tallbear quotes Jonathan Marks, who writes that "'blood' is a *metaphor* for heredity, not heredity itself." I learned that commercial DNA testing (for ancestry at least) is as absurd as the "scratch test" they used to administer to Native folks in the Americas to determine their Native status; they'd scratch the chest of a test taker with the tip of a fingernail to see what color the line of raised, reddening skin turned.

In *Fantasies of Identification*, Samuels writes that ancestry DNA testing is just another way to try to corral something like identity that's unobtainable and unclassifiable—ethnicity and race and gender, for example, which don't live in the body. Some aspects do, sure, but in immeasurable ways.

The book argues that we can look and look for gender in the body and it just will not be there. It explores the story of Caster Semenya, a South African middle-distance runner who was subjected to gender testing following her victory at the 2009 World Championships and who, in 2019, lost a ruling against the International Association of Athletics Federations, which requires athletes with "differences in sexual development (DSD)" to take hormones.

"The IAAF used me in the past as a human guinea pig to experiment with how the medication they required me to take would affect my testosterone levels," Semenya said to news outlets following the ruling. "Even though the hormonal drugs made me feel constantly sick, the IAAF now wants to enforce even stricter thresholds with unknown health consequences."

Semenya's case is a story of expectations.

"Certain bodies are never allowed to be female," said intersex activist Pidgeon Pagonis, co-founder of the Intersex Justice Project. Pagonis was quoted in an article about Semenya published by *Vox*. In the article, Pagonis links expectations of femininity with white supremacy and anti-blackness. "What I think this comes down to is, Caster's faster than white girls and she made them cry."

Samuels writes in *Fantasies of Identification* that "desire for reassurance drives the continuing fantasy of identification based on a definite, incontrovertible measure of sex... Even if full medical details were provided, they would not contain that definitive, single marker of femaleness the fantasy demands because such a marker simply does not exist."

The book concludes that we need to "seek to create a future based more on justice than fantasy..."

And much of its argument springs from the understanding that no physical proof exists in the body to substantiate identity.

But, "to what extent does the body *come into being* in and through the mark(s) of gender?" Judith Butler asks and asks.

I don't remember much about Mom's visit to my place in Brooklyn, I remember the shitty things much more regularly and in color, but I do remember her boyfriend saying to me that he'd had to hold her back from going right then at ten or something at night, had to convince her to wait for the morning.

When I went to visit Mom for the first time after rehab, she'd just moved from the motel into that camper parked on the periphery of the graveyard. I was making a movie with my friend from New

York, she was making it, but I was the star and we wanted to film it in Mom's camper.

It looked like *8 Mile* but set in a graveyard and my friend liked that, we surprised my mom and for the first time ever, I think she was excited. She was excited to see me and she played along. Now there's this clip I have of her opening her screen door and calling out, Baby! Baby! She was supposed to be a worried mother in the film and I was the drunk, it was called *Baby Jim*.

She played it really well. I felt what she was doing go through me. I'd never seen her perform anxiousness about my using or myself at all really.

I loved it, loved smoking outside her trailer and getting to be the bad one for a minute, her worried for me.

In real life, if she'd had this feeling, I wouldn't have let it, I couldn't absorb it, didn't want to. The enormity of it would have been too much. I couldn't have let her be loving because it was too painful, the most painful, my mom.

Now, she sends me photos of things she's making, different animals out of socks or felt and things, and I'm happy for her. She's trained a squirrel to jump onto the head of a statue in her backyard and take a nut from her hand, she walks around with her hands open, her heart open, and when we're alone, I can follow. Just sometimes she talks in her child voice to the guy at the AT&T store and I'm afraid again about how I'm being seen.

Recently, when I was visiting my family outside New York, I found a small paperback on the shelf. It had a strange "as above, so below" chalice on the cover that was drawn into the outline of two heads. I thought it might be something witchy. I picked it up and was shocked to see that it was a worn copy of *Adult Children of Alcoholics* by Janet Woititz, Ed.D., 1983. There's an extremely '80s black-and-white portrait of Janet on the back cover, puffed hair, ruffled collar, she's looking off into the distance with a pensive, hopeful glint.

I opened the book and realized it was full of highlights and notations. Next to certain descriptors ("Gloria was a good little girl who did what she was told") there were cursive names of family members (I presume they were someone's family members) written in ball point in the margins—"mom and cheryl, miki, davey, etc." I don't know anyone with those names, I opened the book to its first highlight on the very first page:

"If a child is like a puppy, you were not a child."

I sat on the edge of the bed in the room and considered it, pictured my childhood self, weirdly mannish, serious. I thought of a phone conversation between Mom and me that went something like:

You know, you've never really felt like my daughter.

I paused.

We were in between conversations about her cat: the cat had wrestled out of its harness (at the time, she was letting her cat outside like a pony in the circus, on a leash, attached to a stake in the backyard. The cat loved it, sat while she put its harness on, rubbed her hand with its face).

I thought she was about to say something about my lack of femininity, about my man-ness or whatever this is, about me in relationship to Ellen DeGeneres or Chaz Bono, was braced for the awkwardness of that.

Instead she said, I've always felt we were more like friends.

I held the phone away from my head and listened to the noise of her voice mop the air around the speaker, she didn't stop talking. I held the phone away from my head at arm's length, she kept talking. I tossed it onto the bed and lay next to it, she was still talking.

This is not friends, I figured.

I was feeling slighted at the time, I'd wanted her to ask about me. I was doing things with my life that I was proud of and wanted to

share. I wanted to interrupt her and say, Hey Mom, I was preg-
nant in my dream last night. The baby that emerged from me was
minuscule and popped from my vagina like a tampon, not fully
cooked, I checked it out like I would anything, then stuck it back
inside myself, knowing it needed to warm longer. Maybe I do want
to be a parent, after all of this.

On Mother's Day this year, she and I had a better phone call,
partially because I'd just called to listen. During the call, she lowered her voice and pressed her lips against the receiver, said softly
toward the end, Do you think heaven could be the best days of
your life on repeat? Do you think when I go to heaven, if I get to
go, I'd go back to those days when all three of you were toddlers
and I was your mom? Do you think heaven could be those times
when we spread the sheet out on the floor while it was so hot?

She says heaven like a little girl asking about heaven. It's like an
accident. Like wetting the bed, the way she says it. Her regret has
mutated into a titanic childishness. I never know what to say.

On our visit last summer, she wanted badly to show me this vernal
spring, a Jesuit spring, she called it. We had to trespass across this
rich woman's property—park almost in her driveway. It was July,
most of the summer people were in their homes, so it seemed likely
that the house was occupied. But she walked us up to it anyway,
talked to me about how this is her favorite house, how she'd love
to live here. I took a breath as I watched her navigate the expensive

place, growing more and more anxious that a twisted face might show up in one of the windows.

She walked right up to a window, pressed her hands against it, looked inside, then called me over. I pretended not to hear, her ruddy body swayed through thigh-high wildflowers.

I didn't move.

They're out of town, she called.

I didn't believe her.

We never made it to the spring. It was high tide, so she couldn't show it to me, but I followed slightly behind her as she climbed the thin sediment away from the dunes. She led me to a small clearing of grass near the shoals.

I saw a baby deer laying here once, she said, sitting down in the grass near a knot of bushes.

It was just like this, she said, putting her head on her hands, curling her body into a circle.

Come be a baby deer with me! she squealed.

I hesitated. The grass looked muddy, she was wide-eyed.

Come on! she said.

I stuffed my hands in my pockets and sat down in the grass next to her. She smelled like tea and high tide. Tiny gnats made their way into her hair. I brushed at them for her and her breathing lit my hand.

She made a deer noise, like a bleat. She wanted me to lie down, was going to keep bleating. A single leaf fell behind us, she bleated again, looked up at me. I lay down like she wanted.

There you go! she said, like I'd found something.

Who was mothered like they wanted to be?

We listened to the water for a long time, not saying anything. She had her hands clasped under her head, was looking at a line of waves moving at us from a boat.

She said it again: Do you think I'll go to heaven?

I listened to her breathing, mine mixed with hers.

I was supposed to be a deer. I nodded, hoping the sound of my forehead pushing slightly against the grass was enough of an answer.

* * *

When I visited Mom that summer, we sat outside her house watching her cat. She lives in a subsidized housing development where all the houses are pastel. She lives alone, so alone surrounded by houses with plastic playground equipment and small families.

We were sitting on her back porch having sodas and I noticed how nervous I was to be near her, my leg was jogging up and down.

She looked a little pink, like she'd been running but she hadn't been. Her hair was freshly dyed and she was brushing it behind her ears and talking to me, high-pitched and passionate like water falling, tripping into that very particular accent that I can understand and imitate, but no one else seems to be able to.

Sitting in her plastic lawn furniture on the deck, I tried to relax my hands, brought my legs up with me into the cushioned plastic chair. I looked at her profile because she wasn't looking at me. My hair was buzzed on both sides, long on top, but I'd tried to tone down all the LA stuff for her. Mom was wearing fleece and flannel, me too. She hardly looked older, only her hands were aging in a way.

After a few minutes on her porch, she asked me if I'd like to see her outdoor altar.

What?

My outdoor altar! she said, standing up.

Sure, I said. I put my hands in my pockets. She was skipping toward a part of her crescent-shaped yard that backed up against a thin strip of forest, walking us to an edge that seemed thickest with trees. Her back was to me, small brown and black birds blew up around us.

It's my altar to my children, she said over her shoulder.

I followed her under branches, over a spongy hill. She pointed to a small grouping of little statues that she'd gathered beneath a tree. She pointed at each one and explained it in that lilting child's voice, higher pitched than before because she was excited. She squatted next to the statues and looked up at me. Her eyes were so light.

There was a green cartoon frog holding a sunflower pressed into the moss, that's Tye, she said. The other was some kind of smiling woodland animal on a log—Gunner. And I was this somber stone one—a girl wearing overalls, lying on her stomach and reading a book. The girl's face and back were cracked quite a bit—almost in half, a big crack right between her eyes.

It's perfect, I said, because it was.

She pointed at a little metal cross that she'd nailed into a tree above the vignette.

I kneel here in the mornings with my devotional, she said, pointing out a matted place in the grass underneath the tree.

A tight melancholy moved in my throat.

That's great Mom, I said, stuffing my hands in my pockets.

She pointed up at a cardinal bopping across a branch overhead and started cooing to the cat.

Do you see it? she said. Do you see the birdie? She spoke to the cat like no one could hear. The cat watched her finger, switched its tail.

As she led me back to the chairs on her porch, I realized I wanted to tell her about my life—I'd just found out my first book was being published, landed my first teaching job. I opened my mouth to say something about Los Angeles but stopped. Her eyes were darting all around the yard like her cat's, her shoulders were forward, her chin was high. I watched her, took another sip of soda.

She asked if I noticed her hummingbird feeder and I nodded, she'd shown it to me before, made it herself out of something glass and put it on a stake near the porch.

She said we had to be quiet if I wanted to see a hummingbird. Her jaw was set. I jumped my leg up and down. I literally had hundreds of hummingbirds in my yard in Los Angeles. I'd just been on a six-hour flight, a five-hour bus trip, then an hour car ride. I wanted to talk. I listened to her breathing. She sat there with big blue eyes, rubbing her hands together, skin flaking off from chemicals that she used to clean rooms at the inn, watching for just one, at least one, like her cat.

And the longer we sat there, the more her innocence was too much for me. This attention to the birds and the yard, too much, a crazy amount of sweetness. I wished for someone else to glance at. I rubbed my hands together and sat with her silently for another hour or so until it was cold.

Eventually, she sighed and swung her eyes toward me.

I guess they're not coming, she said, so deeply, so sadly.

I'd forgotten what we were doing.

Oh, the hummingbirds, I said.

Her shoulders were bent forward, curving around her face. She looked like she might cry. I was sorry in a way that felt like falling asleep. The light that was hitting her glasses was sharp and sweet. She looked so human. She was a person. She is a person, I kept thinking. She is a person and this is how she loves me. It's okay, I said, soft in the way I said it. I don't need to see a hummingbird, I came to see you.

I guess, she said, looking at her hands in her lap. I guess I'm not supposed to show you my hummingbirds.

We sat there in silence for another few minutes. She was sitting in a chair a few feet away, angled in the other direction, I wanted to put my arm around her, my forearm, her shoulders, I didn't. The light off her body, my body was warm. I didn't need to move.

Mom and I texted a few days ago. She wanted help with iTunes. She wanted to be able to download "Anaconda" by Nikki Minaj and play it on a set of Bluetooth speakers she was looking at online.

you sure it is compatible? what kind of phone do i have again? it is only 27 bucks. i made that today in tips. I'm nervous to push the buy button. thank you for helping me. Also can u do me a favor? check out the trip advisor for the inn... remembering i am in charge of keeping it clean... make sure you read about 10 reviews... i am in charge of cleaning it all, 103 rooms, vry stressful. thank u for ur help.

On TripAdvisor, about ten reviews down, someone called AZace from Northlake gave a five-star review that started off with delight about the comfort of the bedding and the "well equipped" workout room.

"But the person who really blew us away was the housekeeper Marie..."

I read the review from my laptop just before bed, looked over at a row of photographs that I keep near my dresser, one of Hank, Tye, Gunner, and myself, another of Grammy and me in a heart-shaped frame.

"On our second day I told her we would only need towels and shampoo. When I returned, she had made the beds, cleaned the bathroom, and straightened up. I thanked her and said she'd gone above my expectations, she answered with 'well, you're on vacation!' She got it, rather than throwing the towels at us, she appreciated that we were travelers paying peak season dollars and deserved service. Thank you!!"

I looked back at my dresser, no photos of Mom. I don't have any in the house. I put her name in a Google search just to see. There was one hit, a photo on the inn's website:

Each month during our season we vote on and pick an employee that has shown exceptional workmanship, is a team player and offers to the guests an added value. For the month of August, Marie of Housekeeping has won the honor.

Congratulations, Marie! You have done a fabulous job and deserve this award!

In the photo, she's standing on the sweeping lawn of the hotel that overlooks the sea. She's wearing all white aside from her red apron, her hair is pulled back but is messy across her forehead, she's cradling the small plaque against her chest, both hands cupped beneath it. She looks like she's going to skip off.

Truth is, nobody can really hold in a frame.

"'Myself' never coincides with my image; for it is the image which is heavy, motionless, stubborn," writes Roland Barthes, "And 'myself' which is light, divided, dispersed... 'my-self' doesn't hold still."

Honestly, I want to push this book like a photo into the top drawer of your dresser, smiling with my teeth because I love the way, I imagine, you're seeing this.

These days, I take care of this little dog.

Almost five years ago, I picked her up at a trailer home in the middle of some scant woods. A woman in a long house dress passed this tiny dog to me over a clot of older ones who were dancing around a makeshift gate in the lady's kitchen. Here you go, she said, she's all yours.

The dog was brown and gray, matted with crusty eyes, petrified.

She smelled like sour milk, had to be cleaned. I bathed her, cut her hair. She was three years old—the woman told me that she'd been used as a breeder for a puppy mill in Tennessee. They fucked with her probably. Hit her in the head, yanked on her so she'd breed. Kept her in a three by three-foot cage her whole life, the adoption people said.

When I took her to the vet for the first time, I told her story to the tech.

The vet tech paused when I was done.

Just curious, she said. Do you think about her in a kind of sorry way? Like when you pet her?

I looked up because I did do that. I'd try to get her to play and she wouldn't and wouldn't wag and I'd hold her and picture all her pain.

The tech shook her head. Probably time for a new story, she said. Just be present for what happens, enjoy her.

I have taken care of her for all these years now.

I love her, wash her while she presses a tiny nose into my palm.

She gets excited to see no one else, really. Won't let most people touch her.

A few months ago, she started wagging her tail. It just started moving one day as if it always had. This little gray tail shaking against her back. I stepped through the door and she walked up to me, wagging. I dropped to my knees.

I was ecstatic, I still am.

To protect the identities of those in the text, names in *Heaven* have been changed and identifying details have been altered. Certain scenes are intentional composites as a result. *Heaven* was written via recollection, and all inaccuracies are purposefully left uncorrected.

This book uses the word "Gypsy," as my family uses it to refer to their Hungarian-Slovak "Gypsy" background. The word here is a form of reclamation. Generally, it is a slur used against Roma or Romani people. I do not condone the use of the slur.

ACKNOWLEDGMENTS

Parts of this book appeared, in different forms, in *Troubling The Line: Trans and Genderqueer Poetry and Poetics* (thank you Trace Peterson and TC Tolbert) and *Bombay Gin* (thank you Angel Dominguez and JH Phrydas).

A tremendous thank you to Tim Wojcik, whose unwavering support of this book made it possible. Thank you to Claire Boyle for her celebration of this text and her truly luminous editorial direction. It's been a gift to work with you. Thanks to Amanda Uhle for taking a chance on me. Thank you Maggie Nelson for everything.

I also want to thank all those who provided support and inspiration throughout this process. I'm naming a number of folks who I worked with directly during the writing of this book: Iggy Dodge Nelson, Dan Bustillo, Jamila Cornick, Pilar Gallego, Eileen Myles, Sherry Velasco, CA Conrad, Diana Waters, Arisa White, Clay Kerrigan, Emma Kemp, Adriana Wid-does, Joey Cannizzaro, Mady Schutzman, Ebony Williams, Karen Barad, Catherine Malabou, Judith Butler, Katharine Jose, Sandy Hall-Chiles, my cohort at CalArts and at EGS, Jim Lindsay, Tish, Emily, Isabel, Craig, Harry, Chuck, Wayne, Dad, Eric Kosse, Dale and Pat, Gender Justice Los Angeles, TGI Justice, Amanda Cole, Anastasia Baratta, Jen Hofer, Quinn Anex-Ries, Emmett Harmony Drager, Herukhuti Williams, Muriel Shockley, Laurie Foos, Otto Muller, Caitlin Churchill, Wren Warner, Whit Annicelli, Grannie, Grammy and Grandpa, and my mom. I'm so grateful for all of you.

This book is written in loving memory of Peter Kaplan, El Belden, Great Gran, and Carl E.

ABOUT THE AUTHOR

Emerson Whitney is the author of *Ghost Box* (Timeless Infinite Light, 2014). Emerson teaches in the BFA creative writing program at Goddard College and is a postdoctoral fellow in gender studies at the University of Southern California.